A COMPEND
OF THE INSTITUTES
OF THE
CHRISTIAN RELIGION
BY
JOHN CALVIN

Edited by
HUGH T. KERR

D0107914

THE WESTMINSTER PRESS
Philadelphia

11 10 9 8 7

Published by The Westminster Press
®
Philadelphia, Pennsylvania

PRINTED IN THE UNITED STATES OF AMERICA

FOREWORD

Beyond all comparison, Calvin's *Institutes of the Christian Religion* is the supreme theological structure of the Protestant Reformation. As Martin Luther was unquestionably the major prophet of the Reformation, John Calvin was its greatest systematic theologian. Each made his own distinctive mark not only upon the sixteenth century but upon every subsequent generation. And something of the explosive dynamic of the Reformation can be measured by the continuing and ever-widening research into the life and work of the great Reformers.

John Calvin (as his name is known in English; Jean Cauvin in French; Ioannes Calvinus in Latin) was born in 1509 at Noyon, France, a cathedral town midway between the two more celebrated cathedral towns of Amiens and Reims. His father sent him to Paris to study for the priesthood and then to Orléans to study law. But the son was not to be ordained into the Roman Church, though he became the outstanding churchman, next to Luther, in the Protestant Reformation. Nor was he ever to practice the legal profession, though he helped to rewrite the civil law of the city of Geneva, and the Protestant tradition he founded has always been deeply involved in political and social as well as religious and theological matters.

John Calvin was not one to emotionalize about his own religious experience. He tells us almost nothing of his early spiritual pilgrimage. On his deathbed he sighed, "I am a wretched sinner," and he was buried in an unmarked grave. He does mention "a sudden conversion" when he was twenty-five years old, a conversion from medieval Roman Catholicism and the scholastic theology of Thomas Aquinas to the evangelical Reformation views which had already begun to circulate from Luther's Germany throughout central Europe and into Great Britain.

Two years later (1536) he published the first edition of the

Institutes of the Christian Religion, which as textbook and theological system had a formative influence on the whole development
of Reformed (as distinct from Lutheran) Protestantism. Going
through a dozen revisions and editions, the *Institutes* has been
translated into many languages and is still being translated. Between the first (1536) and the last edition (1559), Calvin was
also publishing tracts and essays of all kinds, and writing com-
mentaries on nearly every book of the Bible. All this time he was
preaching constantly (many manuscript sermons have not yet
been edited), and he was carrying on an extensive correspond-
ence with everyone of any importance in the Church and in
public life and with countless lesser-known persons (about four
thousand letters remain).

Calvin's personality has always been a lively subject for debate.
Calvin the theologian, the scholar, the preacher, the churchman
was also a human being—though his detractors have questioned
even that. His critics have accused him of being overly stern and
severe, headstrong and stubborn, intolerant and cheerless. If the
stereotyped German tends to be stolid, then in some things Calvin
was perhaps more German than was Luther; if the Frenchman is
debonair, then in spite of his birthplace and his native tongue
Calvin scarcely qualifies.

Whether Calvin is the sort of man to elicit friendly affection or
not—and there has always been division of opinion on this point
—his was a mind entirely bent in the direction of the truth. His
utter devotion of intellect and commitment of heart to God and
the divine purpose in Christ have always won the respect they
deserve and need no more apology today than in those far-off
eruptive days in the Geneva of the sixteenth century.

Unfortunately Calvin's name and theology have been unfavor-
ably linked in the popular mind with two easily misunderstood
doctrines: the sovereignty of God, and election or predestination.
Certainly he had much to say about both; perhaps his fault was to
say too much. It was not in his nature to be soft or evasive with
heretics, recalcitrant citizens, or difficult and divisive doctrines.
He was convinced from the Scriptures and from his own experience that God is sovereign in the process of salvation, that it is
God in Christ who takes the initiative in man's redemption, and
that man has nothing whatever within him or about him deserving
of the divine favor. For Calvin to speak of the sovereignty of God
was not to add still another transcendental attribute, such as om-

nipotence, to the classical definitions of deity, but simply to put
first things first in the order of the gospel.

The one thing that overwhelmed Calvin about the Christian
faith was the good news of God's redemptive approach to sinful
mankind in Jesus Christ. It was because he was so sure of this
that he could talk of total depravity, of man's inability to save
himself, and of God's justification of the sinner through faith in
Christ. Calvin was no misanthrope; his concern was to glorify
God.

Election and predestination, it is important to note, do not
figure in the structure of Calvin's *Institutes* until the end of
Book III, that is, at the conclusion of the major doctrinal section
of the work. Here the discussion arises as a theological consequence of the sovereignty of God. Calvin's doctrine of election is
simply his interpretation of how in fact God seems to operate in
the realization of his redemptive purpose. Calvin was not the first
to discuss this doctrine, though he went farther than either Augustine or the apostle Paul, both of whom he claimed as predeces-
sors for his view. Whatever we may make of this doctrine—for
good or for ill, it seems distinctly uncongenial to the modern
mind—for Calvin it had no melancholy fatalistic flavor but was a
source of joy, assurance, and hope. In the midst of staggering
odds, when it was an open question whether the Genevan Reformation would succeed or be smothered, Calvin and his colleagues
found strength and took courage in the realization that it is God
alone who saves, that there is a divine purpose in Christ which
sinful men cannot thwart, and that come good or evil "the Lord
God omnipotent reigneth."

A look at the various editions of the *Institutes* indicates that
Calvin experimented with different kinds of structures for his
theology. The first edition of 1536 was a small book of only six
chapters. The first three comprised the theological nucleus of the
work and dealt with the Ten Commandments, the Apostles' Creed,
and the Lord's Prayer. This threefold system had already been
employed by Luther in the arrangement of his *Small Catechism*
(1529). Prior to that it had been used by Thomas Aquinas in his
Compendium of Theology (1273). Indeed this particular struc-
tural method goes back to Augustine's *Enchiridion* (421), often
called by its subtitle, "On Faith [Apostles' Creed], Hope [Lord's
Prayer], and Love [Ten Commandments]."

By the time of the final, definitive edition of the *Institutes*

(1559), the work had grown from a small to a very large book, and from six to eighty chapters. The organizing principle for this edition was simply the Apostles' Creed, and as it contains four major articles—God, Christ, Holy Spirit, Church—so Calvin divided the work into four corresponding books. He doubtless regarded his method and structure as adequate, especially for the purpose of doctrinal instruction. ("Instruction" would be a more meaningful translation of the Latin *institutio* in Calvin's title; instead of *Institutes of the Christian Religion,* we could read *Instruction in the Christian Religion.*) Calvin tells us in the Preface to the 1559 edition that his purpose was "to prepare and qualify students of theology for the reading of the divine word, that they may have an easy introduction to it, and be enabled to proceed in it without any obstruction. For I think I have given such a comprehensive summary, and orderly arrangement of all the branches of religion, that, with proper attention, no person will find any difficulty in determining what ought to be the principal objects of his research in the Scripture, and to what end he ought to refer any thing it contains."

The continuing influence of Calvin's *Institutes* upon later theologians and thinkers is incalculable. Though many of his harsher doctrines have been softened, his comprehensive structure of Christian truth has always made its own appeal. Karl Barth, for example, in the first volume of his *Church Dogmatics,* notes approvingly that Calvin's method of interweaving Biblical with doctrinal interpretation in the *Institutes* rightly recognizes the church's perennial responsibility to proclaim the Word of God for each new day and age (I/1, pp. 16 f.). In Emil Brunner's *The Christian Doctrine of God,* which is Vol. I of his *Dogmatics,* he acknowledges as the source of his own system "the theological tradition common to the Church as a whole," the framework of which was "in all essentials adopted by that master of Reformed theology, Calvin" (p. vi). And even Paul Tillich, who might not be expected to find John Calvin theologically congenial, observes that the dialectic between the knowledge of God and the knowledge of man with which the *Institutes* begins "expresses the essence of the method of correlation" which is so central for Tillich's own theology (*Systematic Theology,* I, p. 63).

The fact is, however, that much of Calvin's system as well as much of his polemic against Roman Catholicism is hopelessly outdated and irrelevant for modern thought. Systems as such are under general suspicion in almost every area of life and thought. Sectarian apologetics and abusive anathemas against other traditions are both disallowed in our more ecumenical situation. The reform program initiated in the Roman Catholic Church by Pope John XXIII and Vatican Council II represents a radically different situation and one that Calvin in his day could not have contemplated.

It would be a pity if Calvin's positive Biblical and theological views were ignored simply because they are often entwined with obsolescent arguments and belligerent polemics. Beyond this, the sheer massive bulk of Calvin's 1559 *Institutes* is too overpowering and intimidating. These, then, are some of the reasons for preparing a Compend. The idea is not new. Only twelve years after Calvin's death, there appeared the first in a long series of digests, of which this is one of two or three of recent date.

This Compend, first issued in hard covers some years ago when there was nothing like it in the field, is now presented in paperback format in the hope that it will help to fulfill the contemporary demand of students and others for authentic texts in the original sources of our religious and cultural tradition. The Compend follows the main development of Calvin's theology without lingering over his prolonged attacks on the Roman Church or on matters of only dated importance. The material omitted will be chiefly of interest to Calvin specialists, whereas what is included, though only a tenth of the uncut edition, accentuates Calvin's positive convictions as well as the doctrinal symmetry of the work as a whole.

The selections for this Compend have been made from the English translation of John Allen, which first appeared in 1813 and subsequently in several American editions published by The Westminster Press, Philadelphia, Pa. Calvin's French and Latin are much more lively and idiomatic than Allen's somewhat stiff prose might indicate, but the translation is substantially accurate and the cadence of the lines has its own impressive, if somewhat archaic, quality.

Calvin's table of contents and his chapter headings have been replaced with a simpler, more analytical division, but the sequence of his argument has been maintained throughout. References to the original text are supplied, for purposes of verification and further study, in the margins of the Compend in three figures— e.g., II. iii. 4, the first denoting the book, the second the chapter,

the third the section of the 1559 edition of the *Institutes*. The index
follows the same pattern and includes also the page reference to
the Compend.

A compend, to be sure, can never take the place of the original,
and serious students of Calvin will know that for a complete
understanding of the *Institutes* the unabridged editions must be
consulted, such, for example, as the scholarly and handsome new
English translation in The Library of Christian Classics, edited
by John T. McNeill and translated by Ford Lewis Battles (*Calvin:
Institutes of the Christian Religion,* two volumes, The Westminster Press, 1960, 1734 pp.).

If the Compend succeeds in directing some to the original, that
would be warrant enough for its appearance; if it serves to introduce others to the great evangelical doctrines of the Reformation,
that would be even more desirable. The hope that the Compend
will make Calvin better known prompts this publication. In the
vivid phrase of Philip Schaff, the American Church historian of
a former generation, "the Reformation was a deeper plunge into
the meaning of the Gospel." This Compend is an invitation, and
perhaps a springboard, to make that plunge in our day.

HUGH T. KERR

Princeton Theological Seminary
Princeton, New Jersey
May 27, 1964
    The quatercentenary of Calvin's death

CONTENTS

Book II

THE SIN OF MAN AND JESUS CHRIST THE REDEEMER

Book III

THE HOLY SPIRIT

Book IV

THE HOLY CATHOLIC CHURCH

Book I

God the Creator

CHAPTER I

The Knowledge of God

❧

(1) THE KNOWLEDGE OF GOD AND THE KNOWLEDGE OF OURSELVES

TRUE and substantial wisdom principally consists of two parts, I. i. 1 the knowledge of God, and the knowledge of ourselves. But, while these two branches of knowledge are so intimately connected, which of them precedes and produces the other, is not easy to discover. For, in the first place, no man can take a survey of himself but he must immediately turn to the contemplation of God, in whom he "lives and moves;" (a) since it is evident that the talents which we possess are not from ourselves, and that our very existence is nothing but a subsistence in God alone. These bounties, distilling to us by drops from heaven, form, as it were, so many streams conducting us to the fountain-head. Our poverty conduces to a clearer display of the infinite fulness of God. Especially, the miserable ruin, into which we have been plunged by the defection of the first man, compels us to raise our eyes towards heaven, not only as hungry and famished, to seek thence a supply for our wants, but, aroused with fear, to learn humility. For, since man is subject to a world of miseries, and has been spoiled of his divine array, this melancholy exposure discovers an im-

---

(a) Acts xvii. 2.

3

mense mass of deformity: every one, therefore, must be so impressed with a consciousness of his own infelicity, as to arrive at some knowledge of God. Thus a sense of our ignorance, vanity, poverty, infirmity, depravity, and corruption, leads us to perceive and acknowledge that in the Lord alone are to be found true wisdom, solid strength, perfect goodness, and unspotted righteousness; and so, by our imperfections, we are excited to a consideration of the perfections of God. Nor can we really aspire toward him, till we have begun to be displeased with ourselves. For who would not gladly rest satisfied with himself? where is the man not actually absorbed in self-complacency, while he remains unacquainted with his true situation, or content with his own endowments, and ignorant or forgetful of his own misery? The knowledge of ourselves, therefore, is not only an incitement to seek after God, but likewise a considerable assistance towards finding him.

I. 1. 2   On the other hand, it is plain that no man can arrive at the true knowledge of himself, without having first contemplated the divine character, and then descended to the consideration of his own. For, such is the native pride of us all, we invariably esteem ourselves righteous, innocent, wise, and holy, till we are convinced, by clear proofs, of our unrighteousness, turpitude, folly, and impurity. But we are never thus convinced, while we confine our attention to ourselves, and regard not the Lord, who is the only standard by which this judgment ought to be formed. Because, from our natural proneness to hypocrisy, any vain appearance of righteousness abundantly contents us instead of the reality; and, every thing within and around us being exceedingly defiled, we are delighted with what is least so, as extremely pure, while we confine our reflections within the limits of human corruption. So the eye, accustomed to see nothing but black, judges that to be very white, which is but whitish, or perhaps brown. Indeed, the senses of our bodies may assist us in discovering how grossly we err in estimating the powers of the soul. For if at noonday we look either on the ground, or at any surrounding objects, we conclude our vision to be very strong and piercing; but when we raise our eyes and steadily look at the sun, they are at once dazzled and confounded with such a blaze of brightness, and we are constrained to confess, that our sight, so piercing in viewing terrestrial things, when directed to the sun, is dimness itself. Thus also it happens in the consideration of our spiritual endowments. For as long as our views are bounded by the earth, perfectly content with our own righteousness, wisdom, and strength, we fondly flatter ourselves, and fancy we are little less than demigods. But, if we once elevate our thoughts to God, and consider his nature, and the consummate perfection of his righteousness, wisdom, and strength, to which we ought to be conformed, — what before charmed us in ourselves under the false pretext of righteousness, will soon be loathed as the greatest iniquity; what strangely deceived us under the title of wisdom, will be despised as extreme folly; and what wore the appearance of strength, will be proved to be most wretched impotence. So very remote from the divine purity is what seems in us the highest perfection. . . . But, though the knowledge of God and the knowledge of ourselves I. i. 3 be intimately connected, the proper order of instruction requires us first to treat of the former, and then to proceed to the discussion of the latter. . . .

(2) FAITH THE PREREQUISITE TO THE KNOWLEDGE OF GOD

We cannot with propriety say, there is any knowledge of God I. ii. 1 where there is no religion or piety. . . . Since God is first manifested, both in the structure of the world and in the general tenor of Scripture, simply as the Creator, and afterwards reveals himself in the person of Christ as a Redeemer, hence arises a twofold knowledge of him; of which the former is first to be considered, and the other will follow in its proper place. . . . By piety, I mean a reverence and love of God arising from a knowledge of his benefits. . . .

Cold and frivolous . . . are the speculations of those who em- I. ii. 2 ploy themselves in disquisitions on the essence of God, when it would be more interesting to us to become acquainted with his character, and to know what is agreeable to his nature. For what end is answered by professing, with Epicurus, that there is a God, who, discarding all concern about the world, indulges himself in perpetual inactivity? What benefit arises from the knowledge of a

God with whom we have no concern? Our knowledge of God should rather tend, first, to teach us fear and reverence; and secondly, to instruct us to implore all good at his hand, and to render him the praise of all that we receive. For how can you entertain a thought of God without immediately reflecting, that, being a creature of his formation, you must, by right of creation, be subject to his authority? that you are indebted to him for your life, and that all your actions should be done with reference to him? . . .

The nature of pure and genuine religion . . . consists in faith, united with a serious fear of God, comprehending a voluntary reverence, and producing legitimate worship agreeable to the injunctions of the law. And this requires to be the more carefully remarked, because men in general render to God a formal worship, but very few truly reverence him; while great ostentation in ceremonies is universally displayed, but sincerity of heart is rarely to be found.

CHAPTER II

The Knowledge of God Obscured
in Man

❧

(1) MAN'S NATURAL INSTINCT FOR GOD

W<small>E LAY</small> it down as a position not to be controverted, that the <small>I. iii. 1</small>
human mind, even by natural instinct, possesses some sense of a
Deity. For that no man might shelter himself under the pretext
of ignorance, God hath given to all some apprehension of his
existence, (*f*) the memory of which he frequently and insensibly
renews; so that, as men universally know that there is a God, and
that he is their Maker, they must be condemned by their own
testimony, for not having worshipped him and consecrated their
lives to his service. . . . Cicero observes, there is no nation so
barbarous, no race so savage, as not to be firmly persuaded of the
being of a God. (*g*) . . . Now, since there has never been a
country or family, from the beginning of the world, totally destitute of religion, it is a tacit confession, that some sense of the
Divinity is inscribed on every heart. . . .

It is most absurd, then, to pretend, as is asserted by some, that <small>I. iii. 2</small>
religion was the contrivance of a few subtle and designing men,
a political machine to confine the simple multitude to their duty,

---

(*f*) Rom. i. 20.
(*g*) Cicer. de Natur. Deor. lib. i. Lactant. Inst. lib. iii. cap. 10.

7

while those who inculcated the worship of God on others, were themselves far from believing that any god existed. I confess, indeed, that artful men have introduced many inventions into religion, to fill the vulgar with reverence, and strike them with terror, in order to obtain the greater command over their minds. But this they never could have accomplished, if the minds of men had not previously been possessed of a firm persuasion of the existence of God. . . . All have by nature an innate persuasion of the Divine existence, a persuasion inseparable from their very constitution. . . . Whence we infer, that this is a doctrine, not first to be learned in the schools, but which every man from his birth is self-taught, and which, though many strain every nerve to banish it from them, yet nature itself permits none to forget. . . . The worship of God is . . . the only thing which renders men superior to brutes, and makes them aspire to immortality.

I. iii. 3

(2) THIS INSTINCT OBSCURED BY IGNORANCE AND WICKEDNESS

I. iv. 1

While experience testifies that the seeds of religion are sown by God in every heart, we scarcely find one man in a hundred who cherishes what he has received, and not one in whom they grow to maturity, much less bear fruit in due season. Some perhaps grow vain in their own superstitions, while others revolt from God with intentional wickedness; but all degenerate from the true knowledge of him. The fact is, that no genuine piety remains in the world. . . . We see many, become hardened by bold and habitual transgressions, striving to banish all remembrance of God, which the instinct of nature is still suggesting to their minds. . . . They never think of God but against their inclinations, nor approach him till their reluctance is overcome by constraint; and then they are influenced, not by a voluntary fear, proceeding from reverence of the Divine Majesty, but by a servile and constrained fear, extorted by the divine judgment, which they dread because it is inevitable, at the same time that they hate it. . . .

I. iv. 2

I. iv. 4

That seed, which it is impossible to eradicate, a sense of the existence of a Deity, yet remains; but so corrupted as to produce only the worst of fruits. Yet this is a further proof of what I now contend for, that an idea of God is naturally engraved on the hearts of men, since necessity extorts a confession of it, even from reprobates themselves. In the moment of tranquillity, they facetiously mock the Divine Being, and with loquacious impertinence derogate from his power. But if any despair oppress them, it stimulates them to seek him, and dictates concise prayers, which prove that they are not altogether ignorant of God, but that what ought to have appeared before had been suppressed by obstinacy.

CHAPTER III

The Knowledge of God Obscured in the World

❧

(1) GOD'S MANIFESTATION IN THE WORLD

A<small>S THE</small> perfection of a happy life consists in the knowledge of God, that no man might be precluded from attaining felicity, God hath not only sown in the minds of men the seed of religion, already mentioned, but hath manifested himself in the formation of every part of the world, and daily presents himself to public view, in such a manner, that they cannot open their eyes without being constrained to behold him. His essence indeed is incomprehensible, so that his Majesty is not to be perceived by the human senses; but on all his works he hath inscribed his glory in characters so clear, unequivocal, and striking, that the most illiterate and stupid cannot exculpate themselves by the plea of ignorance. . . . Whithersoever you turn your eyes, there is not an atom of the world in which you cannot behold some brilliant sparks at least of his glory. . . . Of his wonderful wisdom, both heaven and earth contain innumerable proofs; not only those more abstruse things, which are the subjects of astronomy, medicine, and the whole science of physics, but those things which force themselves on the view of the most illiterate of mankind, so that they cannot open their eyes without being constrained to witness them. . . .

Ignorance of . . . sciences prevents no man from such a survey of the workmanship of God, as is more than sufficient to excite his admiration of the Divine Architect. . . . It is evident, that the Lord abundantly manifests his wisdom to every individual on earth. . . .

(2) MAN'S BLINDNESS TO GOD'S MANIFESTATION

But herein appears the vile ingratitude of men. . . . They perceive how wonderfully God works within them, and experience teaches them what a variety of blessings they receive from his liberality, . . . yet they suppress this knowledge in their hearts. . . . In the present day, there are many men of monstrous dispositions, who . . . will not say that they are distinguished from the brutes by chance; but they ascribe it to nature, which they consider as the author of all things, and remove God out of sight. . . . I confess, indeed, that the expression, that nature is God, may be used in a pious sense by a pious mind; but, as it is harsh and inconsistent with strict propriety of speech, nature being rather an order prescribed by God, it is dangerous in matters so momentous, and demanding peculiar caution, to confound the Deity with the inferior course of his works. . . .

Notwithstanding the clear representations given by God in the mirror of his works, both of himself and of his everlasting dominion, such is our stupidity, that, always inattentive to these obvious testimonies, we derive no advantage from them. For, with regard to the structure and very beautiful organization of the world, how few of us are there, who, when lifting up their eyes to heaven, or looking round on the various regions of the earth, direct their minds to the remembrance of the Creator, and do not rather content themselves with a view of his works, to the total neglect of their Author! And with respect to those things that daily happen out of the ordinary course of nature, is it not the general opinion, that men are rolled and whirled about by the blind temerity of fortune, rather than governed by the providence of God? . . . We differ from one another, in that each individual imbibes some peculiarity of error; but we perfectly agree in a universal departure from the one true God, to preposterous trifles.

I. v. 4

I. v. 5

I. v. 11

This disease affects, not only the vulgar and ignorant, but the most eminent, and those who, in other things, discover peculiar sagacity. . . .

I. v. 14   Vain, therefore, is the light afforded us in the formation of the world to illustrate the glory of its Author, which, though its rays be diffused all around us, is insufficient to conduct us into the right way. Some sparks, indeed, are kindled, but smothered before they have emitted any great degree of light. Wherefore the Apostle . . . says, " By faith we understand that the worlds were framed by the word of God; " (d) thus intimating, that the invisible Deity was represented by such visible objects, yet that we have no eyes to discern him, unless they be illuminated through faith by an internal revelation of God. . . . Though the Lord, then, is not destitute of a testimony concerning himself, while with various and most abundant benignity he sweetly allures mankind to a knowledge of him, yet they persist in following their own ways, their pernicious and fatal errors. But whatever deficiency

I. v. 15 of natural ability prevents us from attaining the pure and clear knowledge of God, yet, since that deficiency arises from our own fault, we are left without any excuse. . . . For as soon as a survey of the world has just shown us a deity, neglecting the true God, we set up in his stead the dreams and phantasms of our own brains; and confer on them the praise of righteousness, wisdom, goodness, and power, due to him. We either obscure his daily acts, or pervert them by an erroneous estimate; thereby depriving the acts themselves of their glory, and their Author of his deserved praise.

(d) Heb. xi. 3.

CHAPTER IV

The Knowledge of God Revealed in Scripture

(1) SCRIPTURE THE SOURCE OF OUR KNOWLEDGE OF GOD

Though the light which presents itself to all eyes, both in heaven and in earth, is more than sufficient to deprive the ingratitude of men of every excuse, since God, in order to involve all mankind in the same guilt, sets before them all, without exception, an exhibition of his majesty, delineated in the creatures, — yet we need another and better assistance, properly to direct us to the Creator of the world. Therefore he hath not unnecessarily added the light of his word, to make himself known unto salvation, and hath honoured with this privilege those whom he intended to unite in a more close and familiar connection with himself. . . . For, as persons who are old, or whose eyes are by any means become dim, if you show them the most beautiful book, though they perceive something written, but can scarcely read two words together, yet, by the assistance of spectacles, will begin to read distinctly, — so the Scripture, collecting in our minds the otherwise confused notions of Deity, dispels the darkness, and gives us a clear view of the true God. This, then, is a singular favour, that, in the instruction of the Church, God not only uses mute teachers, but even opens

13

his own sacred mouth; not only proclaims that some god ought to be worshipped, but at the same time pronounces himself to be the Being to whom this worship is due; and not only teaches the elect to raise their view to a Deity, but also exhibits himself as the object of their contemplation. . . . We ought to learn from the Scripture, that God, who created the world, may be certainly distinguished from the whole multitude of fictitious deities. . . . The Scripture discovers God to us as the Creator of the world, and declares what sentiments we should form of him, that we may not be seeking after a deity in a labyrinth of uncertainty.

I. vi. 2 But, whether God revealed himself to the patriarchs by oracles and visions, or suggested, by means of the ministry of men, what should be handed down by tradition to their posterity, it is beyond a doubt that their minds were impressed with a firm assurance of the doctrine, so that they were persuaded and convinced that the information they had received came from God. . . . At length, that the truth might remain in the world in a continual course of instruction to all ages, he determined that the same oracles which he had deposited with the patriarchs should be committed to public records. With this design the Law was promulgated, to which the Prophets were afterwards annexed, as its interpreters. . . . This, then, must be considered as a fixed principle, that . . . no man can have the least knowledge of true and sound doctrine, without having been a disciple of the Scripture. . . .

I. vi. 3 God, foreseeing the inefficacy of his manifestation of himself in the exquisite structure of the world, hath afforded the assistance of his word to all those to whom he determined to make his instructions effectual, — if we seriously aspire to a sincere contemplation of God, it is necessary for us to pursue this right way. We must come, I say, to the word, which contains a just and lively description of God as he appears in his works. . . . If we deviate from it, . . . though we run with the utmost celerity, yet, being out of the course, we shall never reach the goal. For it must be concluded, that the light of the Divine countenance, which even the Apostle says " no man can approach unto," (j) is like an inexplicable labyrinth to us, unless we are directed by the line of the

(j) 1 Tim. vi. 16.

word. . . . Therefore the . . . Psalmist, having said, that "the   I. vi. 4
heavens declare the glory of God, and the firmament showeth his
handy-work; day unto day uttereth speech, and night unto night
showeth knowledge," (*l*) afterwards proceeds to the mention of
the word: "The law of the Lord is perfect, converting the soul:
the testimony of the Lord is sure, making wise the simple: the
statutes of the Lord are right, rejoicing the heart: the commandment of the Lord is pure, enlightening the eyes." . . .

(2) THE AUTHORITY OF SCRIPTURE AND THE INTERNAL TESTIMONY OF THE HOLY SPIRIT

Before I proceed any further, it is proper to introduce some   I. vii. 1
remarks on the authority of the Scripture. . . . The subject, indeed, merits a diffuse discussion, and a most accurate examination.
. . . There has very generally prevailed a most pernicious error,
that the Scriptures have only so much weight as is conceded to
them by the suffrages of the Church; as though the eternal and
inviolable truth of God depended on the arbitrary will of men.
For thus, with great contempt of the Holy Spirit, they inquire,
Who can assure us that God is the author of them? Who can with
certainty affirm, that they have been preserved safe and uncor-
rupted to the present age? Who can persuade us that this book
ought to be received with reverence, and that expunged from the
sacred number, unless all these things were regulated by the deci-
sions of the Church? It depends, therefore, (say they,) on the
determination of the Church. . . . How will the impious ridicule   I. vii. 2
our faith, and all men call it in question, if it be understood to
possess only a precarious authority depending on the favour of
men! . . . If the Christian Church has been from the beginning
founded on the writings of the prophets and the preaching of the
apostles, wherever that doctrine is found, the approbation of it
has certainly preceded the formation of the Church; since without
it the Church itself had never existed. . . . When the Church receives it, and seals it with her suffrage, she does not authenticate
a thing otherwise dubious or controvertible; but, knowing it to be

---

(*l*) Ps. xix. 1, &c.

the truth of her God, performs a duty of piety, by treating it with immediate veneration. But, with regard to the question, How shall we be persuaded of its divine original, unless we have recourse to the decree of the Church? this is just as if any one should inquire, How shall we learn to distinguish light from darkness, white from black, sweet from bitter? For the Scripture exhibits as clear evidence of its truth, as white and black things do of their colour, or sweet and bitter things of their taste. . . . Thus the authority of the Church is an introduction to prepare us for the faith of the Gospel. . . .

I. vii. 3

I. vii. 4

It must be maintained, as I have before asserted, that we are not established in the belief of the doctrine till we are indubitably persuaded that God is its Author. The principal proof, therefore, of the Scriptures is every where derived from the character of the Divine Speaker. The prophets and apostles boast not of their own genius, or any of those talents which conciliate the faith of the hearers; nor do they insist on arguments from reason; but bring forward the sacred name of God, to compel the submission of the whole world. . . . This persuasion must be sought from a higher source than human reasons, or judgments, or conjectures — even from the secret testimony of the Spirit. . . . Though any one vindicates the sacred word of God from the aspersions of men, yet this will not fix in their hearts that assurance which is essential to true piety. Religion appearing, to profane men, to consist wholly in opinion, in order that they may not believe any thing on foolish or slight grounds, they wish and expect it to be proved by rational arguments, that Moses and the prophets spake by divine inspiration. But I reply, that the testimony of the Spirit is superior to all reason. For as God alone is a sufficient witness of himself in his own word, so also the word will never gain credit in the hearts of men, till it be confirmed by the internal testimony of the Spirit. It is necessary, therefore, that the same Spirit, who spake by the mouths of the prophets, should penetrate into our hearts, to convince us that they faithfully delivered the oracles which were divinely intrusted to them. . . .

I. vii. 5

They who have been inwardly taught by the Spirit, feel an entire acquiescence in the Scripture, and that it is self-authenticated, carrying with it its own evidence, and ought not to be made the subject of demonstration and arguments from reason; but it obtains the credit which it deserves with us by the testimony of the Spirit. For though it conciliate our reverence by its internal majesty, it never seriously. affects us till it is confirmed by the Spirit in our hearts. Therefore, being illuminated by him, we now believe the divine original of the Scripture, not from our own judgment or that of others, but we esteem the certainty, that we have received it from God's own mouth by the ministry of men, to be superior to that of any human judgment, and equal to that of an intuitive perception of God himself in it. . . . It is such a persuasion, therefore, as requires no reasons; such a knowledge as is supported by the highest reason, in which, indeed, the mind rests with greater security and constancy than in any reasons; it is, finally, such a sentiment as cannot be produced but by a revelation from heaven. I speak of nothing but what every believer experiences in his heart, except that my language falls far short of a just explication of the subject. . . . That alone is true faith which the Spirit of God seals in our hearts. . . .

Whenever, therefore, we are disturbed at the paucity of believers, let us, on the other hand, remember that none, but those to whom it was given, have any apprehension of the mysteries of God. . . . The Scripture will . . . only be effectual to produce I. viii. 13 the saving knowledge of God, when the certainty of it shall be founded on the internal persuasion of the Holy Spirit. . . . Human testimonies, which contribute to its confirmation, will not be useless, if they follow that first and principal proof, as secondary aids to our imbecility. But those persons betray great folly, who wish it to be demonstrated to infidels that the Scripture is the word of God, which cannot be known without faith. Augustine therefore justly observes, (m) that piety and peace of mind ought to precede, in order that a man may understand somewhat of such great subjects.

(3) THE ADEQUACY OF SCRIPTURE

Persons who, abandoning the Scripture, imagine to themselves I. ix. 1 some other way of approaching to God, must be considered as not

---

(m) Lib. de Util. Credend.

so much misled by error as actuated by frenzy. For there have lately arisen some unsteady men, who, haughtily pretending to be taught by the Spirit, reject all reading themselves, and deride the simplicity of those who still attend to (what they style) the dead and killing letter. . . . How diabolical . . . is that madness which pretends that the use of the Scripture is only transient and temporary! . . . The office of the Spirit, . . . which is promised to us, is not to feign new and unheard of revelations, or to coin a new system of doctrine, which would seduce us from the received doctrine of the Gospel, but to seal to our minds the same doctrine which the Gospel delivers.

I. ix. 2   Hence we readily understand that it is incumbent on us diligently to read and attend to the Scripture, if we would receive any advantage or satisfaction from the Spirit of God. . . . He is the author of the Scriptures; he cannot be mutable and inconsistent with himself. He must therefore perpetually remain such as he has there discovered himself to be. This is not disgraceful to him; unless we esteem it honourable for him to alter and degenerate

I. ix. 3   from himself. . . . For the Lord hath established a kind of mutual connection between the certainty of his word and of his Spirit. . . . God did not publish his word to mankind for the sake of momentary ostentation, with a design to destroy or annul it immediately on the advent of the Spirit; but he afterwards sent the same Spirit, by whose agency he had dispensed his word, to complete his work by an efficacious confirmation of that word. In this manner Christ opened the understanding of his two disciples; (w) not that, rejecting the Scriptures, they might be wise enough of themselves, but that they might understand the Scriptures. . . . What answer can be given to these things, by those proud fanatics, who think themselves possessed of the only valuable illumination, when, securely neglecting and forsaking the Divine word, they, with equal confidence and temerity, greedily embrace every reverie which their distempered imaginations may have conceived? A very different sobriety becomes the children of God; who, while they are sensible that, exclusively of the Spirit of God, they are utterly destitute of the light of truth, yet are not ig-

---

(w) Luke xxiv. 27, &c.

norant that the word is the instrument, by which the Lord dis-
penses to believers the illumination of his Spirit. For they know no
other Spirit than that who dwelt in and spake by the apostles; by
whose oracles they are continually called to the hearing of the
word. . . .

CHAPTER V

The Nature and Attributes of God

❧

I. x. 1   At present . . . let it suffice to understand how God, the former of heaven and earth, governs the world which he hath made. Both his paternal goodness, and the beneficent inclinations of his will, are every where celebrated; and examples are given of his severity, which discover him to be the righteous punisher of iniquities, especially where his forbearance produces no salutary effects upon the obstinate. . . .

I. x. 2   Moses . . . certainly appears to have intended a brief comprehension of all that it was possible for men to know concerning him — "The Lord, the Lord God, merciful and gracious, long suffering, and abundant in goodness and truth, keeping mercy for thousands, forgiving iniquity, and transgression, and sin, and that will by no means clear the guilty; visiting the iniquity of the fathers upon the children, and upon the children's children." (y) Where we may observe, first, the assertion of his eternity and self-existence, in that magnificent name, which is twice repeated; and secondly, the celebration of his attributes, giving us a description, not of what he is in himself, but of what he is to us, that our knowledge of him may consist rather in a lively perception, than in vain and airy speculation. Here we find an enumeration of the same perfections which, as we have remarked, are illustriously displayed both in heaven and on earth — clemency, goodness, mercy, justice, judgment, and truth. . . . But, to avoid the necessity of

---

(y) Exod. xxxiv. 6.

20

quoting many passages, let us content ourselves at present with referring to one Psalm; (z) which contains such an accurate summary of all his perfections, that nothing seems to be omitted. . . .

These three things it is certainly of the highest importance for us to know — mercy, in which alone consists all our salvation; judgment, which is executed on the wicked every day, and awaits them in a still heavier degree to eternal destruction; righteousness, by which the faithful are preserved, and most graciously supported. . . . Nor is this representation chargeable with an omission of his truth, or his power, or his holiness, or his goodness. For how could we have that knowledge, which is here required, of his righteousness, mercy, and judgment, unless it were supported by his inflexible veracity? And how could we believe that he governed the world in judgment and justice, if we were ignorant of his power? And whence proceeds his mercy, but from his goodness? . . .

(z) Psalm cxlv.

CHAPTER VI

The Trinity

❧

(1) THE DOCTRINE STATED

I. xiii. 2 WHILE [God] . . . declares himself to be but One, he proposes himself to be distinctly considered in Three Persons, without apprehending which, we have only a bare and empty name of God floating in our brains, without any idea of the true God. Now, that no one may vainly dream of three gods, or suppose that the simple essence of God is divided among the Three Persons, we must seek for a short and easy definition, which will preserve us from all error. . . . There are in God three *hypostases;* . . . the Latins have expressed the same thing by the word *person.* . . . If we wish to translate word for word, we may call it *subsistence.* Many, in the same sense, have called it *substance.* Nor has the word *person* been used by the Latins only; but the Greeks also. . . . But both Greeks and Latins, notwithstanding any verbal difference, are in perfect harmony respecting the doctrine itself.

I. xiii. 3 Now, though heretics rail at the word *person,* . . . how very unreasonable is it to reprobate words which express nothing but what is testified and recorded in the Scriptures! It were better, say they, to restrain not only our thoughts, but our expressions also, within the limits of the Scripture, than to introduce exotic words, which may generate future dissensions and disputes; for thus we weary ourselves with verbal

22

controversies; thus the truth is lost in altercation; thus charity expires in odious contention. If they call every word exotic, which cannot be found in the Scriptures in so many syllables, they impose on us a law which is very unreasonable, and which condemns all interpretation, but what is composed of detached texts of Scripture connected together. . . . We should seek in the Scriptures a certain rule, both for thinking and for speaking; by which we may regulate all the thoughts of our minds, and all the words of our mouths. But what forbids our expressing, in plainer words, those things which, in the Scriptures, are, to our understanding, intricate and obscure, provided our expressions religiously and faithfully convey the true sense of the Scripture, and are used with modest caution, and not without sufficient occasion? . . .

If, then, the words have not been rashly invented, we should I. xiii. 5 beware lest we be convicted of fastidious temerity in rejecting them. I could wish them, indeed, to be buried in oblivion, provided this faith were universally received, that the Father, Son, and Holy Spirit, are the one God; and that nevertheless the Son is not the Father, nor the Spirit the Son, but that they are distinguished from each other by some peculiar property. I am not so rigidly precise as to be fond of contending for mere words. For I observe that the ancients, who otherwise speak on these subjects with great piety, are not consistent with each other, nor, in all cases, with themselves. . . . If any persons are prevented . . . from admitting these terms, yet not one of them can deny, that, when the Scripture speaks of one God, it should be understood of a unity of substance; and that, when it speaks of three in one essence, it denotes the Persons in this trinity. When this is honestly confessed, we have no further concern about words. . . .

(2) THE DISTINCTION BETWEEN THE PERSONS

But, leaving the dispute about terms, I shall now enter on the I. xiii. 6 discussion of the subject itself. What I denominate a Person, is a subsistence in the Divine essence, which is related to the others, and yet distinguished from them by an incommunicable property. By the word *subsistence* we mean something different from the word *essence*. For, if the *Word* were simply God, and had no peculiar property, John had been guilty of impropriety in saying that he was always *with God*. (*l*) When he immediately adds, that *the Word* also *was God*, he reminds us of the unity of the essence. But because he could not be *with God*, without subsisting in the Father, hence arises that subsistence, which, although inseparably connected with the essence, has a peculiar mark, by which it is distinguished from it. Now, I say that each of the three subsistences has a relation to the others, but is distinguished from them by a peculiar property. We particularly use the word *relation*, (or *comparison*,) here, because, when mention is made simply and indefinitely of God, this name pertains no less to the Son and Spirit, than to the Father. But whenever the Father is compared with the Son, the property peculiar to each distinguishes him from the other. Thirdly, whatever is proper to each of them, I assert to be incommunicable, because whatever is ascribed to the Father as a character of distinction, cannot be applied or transferred to the Son. Nor, indeed, do I disapprove of the definition of Tertullian, if rightly understood: " That there is in God a certain distribution or economy, which makes no change in the unity of the essence." . . .

I. xiii. 17   We find in the Scriptures a distinction between the Father and the Word, between the Word and the Spirit; in the discussion of which the magnitude of the mystery reminds us that we ought to proceed with the utmost reverence and sobriety. I am exceedingly pleased with this observation of Gregory Nazianzen: " I cannot think of the *one*, but I am immediately surrounded with the splendour of the *three*; nor can I clearly discover the *three*, but I am suddenly carried back to the *one*." Wherefore let us not imagine such a trinity of Persons, as includes an idea of separation, or does not immediately recall us to the unity. The names of Father, Son, and Spirit, certainly imply a real distinction; let no one suppose them to be mere epithets, by which God is variously designated from his works; but it is a distinction, not a division. . . . The Son has a property, by which he is distinguished from the Father; because the Word had not been with God, or had his glory with the Father, unless he had been distinct from him. He likewise distinguishes

---

(*l*) John i. 1.

the Father from himself. . . . Besides, the Father descended not to the earth, but he who came forth from the Father. The Father neither died nor rose again, but he who was sent by the Father. . . . The distinction between the Holy Spirit and the Father is announced by Christ, when he says, that he " proceedeth from the Father." (g) But how often does he represent him as another, distinct from himself! as when he promises that " another Comforter " (h) should be sent, and in many other places.

(3) THE DOCTRINE EXPLAINED

I doubt the propriety of borrowing similitudes from human **I. xiii. 18** things, to express the force of this distinction. . . . Yet it is not right to be silent on the distinction which we find expressed in the Scriptures; which is this — that to the Father is attributed the principle of action, the fountain and source of all things; to the Son, wisdom, counsel, and the arrangement of all operations; and the power and efficacy of the action is assigned to the Spirit. Moreover, though eternity belongs to the Father, and to the Son and Spirit also, since God can never have been destitute of his wisdom or his power, and in eternity we must not inquire after any thing prior or posterior, — yet the observation of order is not vain or superfluous, while the Father is mentioned as first; in the next place the Son, as from him; and then the Spirit, as from both. For the mind of every man naturally inclines to the consideration, first, of God; secondly, of the wisdom emanating from him; and lastly, of the power by which he executes the decrees of his wisdom. For this reason the Son is said to be from the Father, and the Spirit from both the Father and the Son. . . . " These distinctive appellations," says Augustine, " denote their **I. xiii. 19** reciprocal relations to each other, and not the substance itself, which is but one." . . . Augustine, in another place, admirably and perspicuously explains the cause of this diversity, in the following manner: " Christ, considered in himself, is called God; but with relation to the Father, he is called the Son." And again, " The Father, considered in himself, is called God; but with re-

---

(g) John xv. 26.   (h) John xiv. 16.

lation to the Son, he is called the Father. He who, with relation to the Son, is called the Father, is not the Son; he who, with relation to the Father, is called the Son, is not the Father; they who are severally called the Father and the Son, are the same God." . . .

I. xiii. 20   Therefore, let such as love sobriety, and will be contented with the measure of faith, briefly attend to what is useful to be known; which is, that, when we profess to believe in one God, the word *God* denotes a single and simple essence, in which we comprehend three Persons, or hypostases; and that, therefore, whenever the word *God* is used indefinitely, the Son and Spirit are intended as much as the Father; but when the Son is associated with the Father, that introduces the reciprocal relation of one to the other; and thus

I. xiii. 22   we distinguish between the Persons. . . . We maintain . . . that the essence of the one God, which pertains to the Father, to the Son, and to the Spirit, is simple and undivided, and, on the other hand, that the Father is, by some property, distinguished from the

I. xiii. 29   Son, and likewise the Son from the Spirit. . . . I trust that the whole substance of this doctrine has been faithfully stated and explained, provided my readers set bounds to their curiosity, and are not unreasonably fond of tedious and intricate controversies. For I have not the least expectation of giving satisfaction to those who are pleased with an intemperance of speculation. . . .

CHAPTER VII

The Creation of the World

❧

(1) THE CREATOR AND CREATION

GREAT shrewdness was discovered by a certain pious old man, I. xiv. 1
who, when some scoffer ludicrously inquired what God had been
doing before the creation of the world, replied that he had been
making hell for over curious men. . . . To apprehend . . . what I. xiv. 20
it is for our benefit to know concerning God, we must first of all
understand the history of the creation of the world. . . . Thence
we shall learn that God, by the power of his Word and Spirit,
created out of nothing the heaven and the earth; that from them
he produced all things, animate and inanimate; distinguished by
an admirable gradation the innumerable variety of things; to
every species gave its proper nature, assigned its offices, and appointed its places and stations; and since all things are subject to
corruption, has, nevertheless, provided for the preservation of
every species till the last day; that he therefore nourishes some
by methods concealed from us, from time to time infusing, as it
were, new vigor into them; that on some he has conferred the
power of propagation, in order that the whole species may not be
extinct at their death; that he has thus wonderfully adorned
heaven and earth with the utmost possible abundance, variety, and
beauty, like a large and splendid mansion, most exquisitely and
copiously furnished; lastly, that, by creating man, and distinguish-

ing him with such splendid beauty, and with such numerous and great privileges, he has exhibited in him a most excellent specimen of all his works. But since it is not my design to treat at large of the creation of the world, let it suffice to have again dropped these few hints by the way. . . .

I. xiv. 21   If we wished to explain how the inestimable wisdom, power, justice, and goodness, of God are manifested in the formation of the world, no splendour or ornament of diction will equal the magnitude of so great a subject. . . . But, this being a didactic treatise, we must omit those topics which require long declamations. To be brief, therefore, let the readers know, that they have then truly apprehended by faith what is meant by God being the Creator of heaven and earth, if they, in the first place, follow this universal rule, not to pass over, with ungrateful inattention or oblivion, those glorious perfections which God manifests in his creatures, and, secondly, learn to make such an application to themselves as thoroughly to affect their hearts. The first point is exemplified, when we consider how great must have been the Artist who disposed that multitude of stars, which adorn the heaven, in such a regular order, that it is impossible to imagine any thing more beautiful to behold. . . . So, also, when we observe his power in sustaining so great a mass, in governing the rapid revolutions of the celestial machine, and the like. . . . Were I desirous of pursuing the subject to its full extent, there would be no end; since there are as many miracles of Divine power, as many monuments of Divine goodness, as many proofs of Divine wisdom, as there are species of things in the world, and even as there are individual things, either great or small.

(2) THE RELIGIOUS SIGNIFICANCE
OF CREATION

I. xiv. 22   There remains the other point, which approaches more nearly to faith; that, while we observe how God has appointed all things for our benefit and safety, and at the same time perceive his power and grace in ourselves, and the great benefits which he has conferred on us, we may thence excite ourselves to confide in him, to invoke him, to praise him, and to love him. . . . Whenever we call God the Creator of heaven and earth, let us at the same time reflect, that the dispensation of all those things which he has made is in his own power, and that we are his children, whom he has received into his charge and custody, to be supported and educated; so that we may expect every blessing from him alone, and cherish a certain hope that he will never suffer us to want those things which are necessary to our well-being, that our hope may depend on no other; that, whatever we need or desire, our prayers may be directed to him, and that, from whatever quarter we receive any advantage, we may acknowledge it to be his benefit, and confess it with thanksgiving; that, being allured with such great sweetness of goodness and beneficence, we may study to love and worship him with all our hearts.

CHAPTER VIII

The Creation of Man

❧

(1) THE IMAGE OF GOD IN MAN

I. xv. 1 WE MUST now treat of the creation of man, not only because he exhibits the most noble and remarkable specimen of the Divine justice, wisdom, and goodness, among all the works of God, but because, as we observed in the beginning, we cannot attain to a clear and solid knowledge of God, without a mutual acquaintance with ourselves. . . . We shall content ourselves at present with a description of human nature in its primitive integrity. And, indeed, before we proceed to the miserable condition in which man is now involved, it is necessary to understand the state in which he was first created. . . . We shall afterwards, in the proper place, see how far men are fallen from that purity which was bestowed upon Adam. . . .

I. xv. 2 That man consists of soul and body, ought not to be controverted. By the "soul" I understand an immortal, yet created essence, which is the nobler part of him. . . . Though the glory of

I. xv. 3 God is displayed in his external form, yet there is no doubt that the proper seat of his image is in the soul. I admit that external form, as it distinguishes us from brutes, also exalts us more nearly to God; nor will I too vehemently contend with any one who would understand, by the image of God, that

30

"—— while the mute creation downward bend
Their sight, and to their earthly mother tend,
Man looks aloft, and with erected eyes
Beholds his own hereditary skies." (y)

Only let it be decided that the image of God, which appears or
sparkles in these external characters, is spiritual. . . . There is
no small controversy concerning " image " and " likeness " among
expositors who seek for a difference, whereas in reality there is
none, between the two words; " likeness " being only added by
way of explanation. . . . The image of God . . . denotes the
integrity which Adam possessed, when he was endued with a right
understanding, when he had affections regulated by reason, and
all his senses governed in proper order, and when, in the excel-
lency of his nature, he truly resembled the excellence of his
Creator. . . .

No complete definition of this image, however, appears yet to **I. xv. 4**
be given, unless it be more clearly specified in what faculties man
excels, and in what respects he ought to be accounted a mirror
of the Divine glory. But that cannot be better known from any
thing, than from the reparation of his corrupted nature. There is
no doubt that Adam, when he fell from his dignity, was by this
defection alienated from God. Wherefore, although we allow that
the Divine image was not utterly annihilated and effaced in him,
yet it was so corrupted that whatever remains is but horrible deformity. And therefore the beginning of our recovery and salvation is the restoration which we obtain through Christ, who on
this account is called the second Adam; because he restores us
to true and perfect integrity. . . . This is the end of regeneration,
that Christ may form us anew in the image of God. . . . (c) . . .
Now, we may see what Paul comprehends in this renovation. In the
first place, he mentions knowledge, and in the next place, sincere
righteousness and holiness; whence we infer, that in the beginning
the image of God was conspicuous in the light of the mind, in the
rectitude of the heart, and in the soundness of all the parts of our
nature. . . .

(y) Ovid's Metam. lib. l. Dryden's Translation.
(c) Col. iii. 10 [cf. Eph. iv. 24].

(2) THE ERROR OF PANTHEISM

I. xv. 5   But, before I proceed any further, it is necessary to combat the Manichæan error, which Servetus has attempted to revive and propagate in the present age. Because God is said to have breathed into man the breath of life, (h) they supposed that the soul was an emanation from the substance of God; as though some portion of the infinite Deity had been conveyed into man. But it may be easily and briefly shown how many shameful and gross absurdities are the necessary consequences of this diabolical error. For if the soul of man be an emanation from the essence of God, it will follow that the Divine nature is not only mutable and subject to passions, but also to ignorance, desires, and vices of every kind. Nothing is more inconstant than man, because his soul is agitated and variously distracted by contrary motions; he frequently mistakes through ignorance; he is vanquished by some of the smallest temptations; we know that the soul is the receptacle of every kind of impurity; — all which we must ascribe to the Divine nature, if we believe the soul to be part of the essence of God, or a secret influx of the Deity. Who would not dread such a monstrous tenet? It is a certain truth, quoted by Paul from Aratus, that " we are the offspring of God," but in quality, not in substance; forasmuch as he has adorned us with Divine endowments. (i) But to divide the essence of the Creator, that every creature may possess a part of it, indicates extreme madness. It must therefore be concluded beyond all doubt, notwithstanding the Divine image is impressed on the souls of men, that they were no less created than the angels. And creation is not a transfusion, but an origination of existence from nothing. . . .

(3) THE NATURE OF THE SOUL

I. xv. 6
I. xv. 7   It would be folly to seek for a definition of the soul from the heathen philosophers, . . . because the philosophers, being ignorant of the corruption of nature proceeding from the punishment of the fall, improperly confound two very different states of

---

(h) Gen. ii. 7.   (i) Acts xvii. 28.

mankind. Let us, therefore, submit the following division — that
the human soul has two faculties which relate to our present design, the understanding and the will. Now, let it be the office of
the understanding to discriminate between objects, as they shall
respectively appear deserving of approbation or disapprobation;
but of the will, to choose and follow what the understanding shall
have pronounced to be good; to abhor and avoid what it shall have
condemned. . . . Without perplexing ourselves with unnecessary
questions, it should be sufficient for us to know that the understanding is, as it were, the guide and governor of the soul; that the
will always respects its authority, and waits for its judgment in its
desires. . . . Here we only intend to show that no power can be
found in the soul, which may not properly be referred to one or
the other of those two members. . . . God has furnished the soul   I. xv. 8
of man, therefore, with a mind capable of discerning good from
evil, and just from unjust; and of discovering, by the light of
reason, what ought to be pursued or avoided. . . . To this he has
annexed the will, on which depends the choice. The primitive condition of man was ennobled with those eminent faculties. . . . In
this integrity man was endued with free will, by which, if he had
chosen, he might have obtained eternal life. For here it would be
unreasonable to introduce the question respecting the secret predestination of God, because we are not discussing what might
possibly have happened or not, but what was the real nature of
man. Adam, therefore, could have stood if he would, since he fell
merely by his own will. . . . Man, at his first creation, was very
different from all his posterity, who deriving their original from
him in his corrupted state, have contracted an hereditary defile-
ment. . . . But to expostulate with God . . . why he did not sustain him with the power of perseverance, remains concealed in his
mind; . . . it is our duty to restrain our investigations within the
limits of sobriety. . . .

CHAPTER IX

Providence

(1) PROVIDENCE OPPOSED TO FORTUNE, FATE, AND CHANCE

I. xvi. 1 TO REPRESENT God as a Creator only for a moment, who entirely finished all his work at once, were frigid and jejune. . . . When [faith] . . . has learned that he is the Creator of all things, it should immediately conclude that he is also their perpetual governor and preserver; and that not by a certain universal motion, actuating the whole machine of the world, and all its respective parts, but by a particular providence sustaining, nourishing, and providing for everything which he has made. (*m*) . . . All the parts of the world are quickened by the secret inspiration of God. . . .

I. xvi. 2 The providence of God, as it is taught in Scripture, is opposed to fortune and fortuitous accidents. Now, since it has been the common persuasion in all ages, and is also in the present day almost the universal opinion, that all things happen fortuitously, it is certain that every correct sentiment concerning providence is not only obscured, but almost buried in oblivion by this erroneous notion. If any one falls into the hands of robbers, or meets with wild beasts; if by a sudden storm he is shipwrecked on the ocean;

(*m*) Matt. vi. 26, x. 29.

if he is killed by the fall of a house or a tree; if another, wandering through deserts, finds relief for his penury, or, after having been tossed about by the waves, reaches the port, and escapes, as it were, but a hair's-breadth from death, — carnal reason will ascribe all these occurrences, both prosperous and adverse, to fortune. But whoever has been taught from the mouth of Christ, that the hairs of his head are all numbered, (r) will seek further for a cause, and conclude that all events are governed by the secret counsel of God. . . . And, indeed, God asserts his possession of omnipotence, and claims our acknowledgment of this attribute . . . not because he is able to act, yet sits down in idleness, or continues by a general instinct the order of nature originally appointed by him; but because he governs heaven and earth by his providence, and regulates all things in such a manner that nothing happens but according to his counsel. . . . Not a sparrow of the least value falls to the ground without the will of the Father. (d) Certainly, if the flight of birds be directed by the unerring counsel of God, we must be constrained to confess with the Prophet, that, though " he dwelleth on high," yet " he humbleth himself to behold the things which are in heaven and in the earth." (e) . . . I. xvi. 3

I. xvi. 5

Though we are averse to all contentions about words, yet we admit not the term *fate*. . . . For we do not, with the Stoics, imagine a necessity arising from a perpetual concatenation and intricate series of causes, contained in nature; but we make God the Arbiter and Governor of all things, who, in his own wisdom, has, from the remotest eternity, decreed what he would do, and now, by his own power, executes what he has decreed. . . . *Fortune* and *chance* are words of the heathen, with the signification of which the minds of the pious ought not to be occupied. . . . I. xvi. 8

Yet, since the dulness of our minds is very much below the sublimity of the Divine providence, let us endeavour to assist them by a distinction. I say, then, that, notwithstanding the ordination of all things by the certain purpose and direction of God, yet to us they are fortuitous: not that we suppose fortune holds any dominion over the world and mankind, and whirls about all things at random, for such folly ought to be far from the breast of a I. xvi. 9

(r) Matt. x. 30.   (d) Matt. x. 29.   (e) Psalm cxiii. 5, 6.

Christian; but because the order, reason, end, and necessity of events are chiefly concealed in the purpose of God, and not comprehended by the mind of man, those things are in some measure fortuitous, which must certainly happen according to the Divine will. . . .

(2) THE RELIGIOUS SIGNIFICANCE OF PROVIDENCE

I. xvii. 1   As the minds of men are prone to vain subtleties, there is the greatest danger that those who know not the right use of this doctrine will embarrass themselves with intricate perplexities. It will therefore be necessary to touch in a brief manner on the end and design of the Scripture doctrine of the Divine ordination of all things. And here let it be remarked, in the first place, that the providence of God is to be considered as well in regard to futurity, as in reference to that which is past; secondly, that it governs all things in such a manner as to operate sometimes by the intervention of means, sometimes without means, and sometimes in opposition to all means; lastly, that it tends to show the care of God for the whole human race, and especially his vigilance in the government of the Church, which he favours with more particular attention. . . . But we must proceed with modesty, cautious that we call not God to an account at our tribunal; but that we entertain such reverence for his secret judgments, as to esteem his will the

I. xvii. 2   most righteous cause of every thing that he does. . . . None, therefore, will attain just and profitable views of the providence of God, but he who considers that he has to do with his Maker and the Creator of the world, and submits himself to fear and rever-

I. xvii. 3   ence with all becoming humility. . . . Those who have learned this modesty, wiɪɪ neither murmur against God on account of past adversities, nor charge him with the guilt of their crimes. . . . Nor will they . . . put an end to their own lives. . . . Nor will they excuse their flagitious actions by ascribing them to God. . . . But they will rather search the Scripture, to learn what is pleasing to God, that by the guidance of the Spirit they may strive to attain it. . . .

I. xvii. 4   He who has fixed the limits of our life, has also intrusted us with the care of it; has furnished us with means and supplies for its preservation; has also made us provident of dangers; and, that they may not oppress us unawares, has furnished us with cautions and remedies. Now, it is evident what is our duty. If God has committed to us the preservation of our life, we should preserve it; if he offers supplies, we should use them; if he fore-warns us of dangers, we should not rashly run into them; if he furnishes remedies, we ought not to neglect them. . . . The arts of deliberation and caution in men proceed from the inspiration of God, and . . . they subserve the designs of his providence in the preservation of their own lives; as, on the contrary, by neglect and slothfulness, they procure to themselves the evils which he has appointed for them. . . . That man obeys God, who, being   I. xvii. 5 instructed in his will, hastens whither God calls him. . . . God only requires of us conformity to his precepts. If we do any thing contrary to them, it is not obedience, but contumacy and trans-gression. . . .

Book II

The Sin of Man and Jesus Christ the Redeemer

CHAPTER X

Original Sin

(1) THE FACT OF SIN

THERE is much reason in the old adage, which so strongly recom- II. i. 1
mends to man the knowledge of himself. . . . But the knowledge
of ourselves consists, first, in considering what was bestowed on
us at our creation, and the favours we continually receive from
the Divine benignity, that we may know how great the excellence
of our nature would have been, if it had retained its integrity; yet,
at the same time, recollecting that we have nothing properly our
own, may feel our precarious tenure of all that God has conferred on us, so as always to place our dependence upon him.
Secondly, we should contemplate our miserable condition since the
fall of Adam, the sense of which tends to destroy all boasting and
confidence, to overwhelm us with shame, and to fill us with real
humility. . . . This is what the truth of God directs us to seek in II. i. 2
the examination of ourselves: it requires a knowledge that will
abstract us from all confidence in our own ability, deprive us of
every cause of boasting, and reduce us to submission. . . . Without any extraneous support, this very false opinion, that man has
in himself sufficient ability to insure his own virtue and happiness,
generally prevails. . . . Therefore every one who in his preaching
has kindly extolled the excellence of human nature, has received
great applause from almost all ages. . . . Whosoever . . . at-
tends to such teachers as amuse us with a mere exhibition of our

virtues, will make no progress in the knowledge of himself, but will be absorbed in the most pernicious ignorance. . . .

II. 1. 3   We may divide the knowledge man ought to have of himself into these two parts. First, he should consider the end of his being created and endued with such estimable gifts; a reflection which may excite him to the consideration of Divine worship, and of a future life. Secondly, he should examine his own ability, or rather his want of ability, the view of which may confound and almost annihilate him. The former consideration is adapted to acquaint him with his duty, the latter with his power to perform it. . . .

(2) THE NATURE OF SIN

II. 1. 4   We must consider the nature of Adam's sin. . . . The prohibition of the tree of knowledge of good and evil was a test of obedience, that Adam might prove his willing submission to the Divine government. . . . Augustine, indeed, properly observes, that pride was the first of all evils; because, if ambition had not elated man beyond what was lawful and right, he might have continued in his honourable situation. . . . The fall commenced in disobedience. This is . . . confirmed by Paul, who states that all men were ruined by the disobedience of one. (s) . . . If apostasy, which consists in revolting from the government of the Creator, and petulantly rejecting his authority, be a base and execrable crime, it is a vain attempt to extenuate the sin of Adam. . . . Infidelity opened the gate to ambition, and ambition produced obstinacy, so that they cast off the fear of God, and precipitated themselves whithersoever they were led by their lawless desires. . . .

II. 1. 5   As the spiritual life of Adam consisted in a union to his Maker, so an alienation from him was the death of his soul. Nor is it surprising that he ruined his posterity by his defection, which has perverted the whole order of nature in heaven and earth. . . . When the Divine image in him was obliterated, and he was punished with the loss of wisdom, strength, sanctity, truth, and righteousness, with which he had been adorned, but which were suc-

---

(s) Rom. v. 19.

ceeded by the dreadful pests of ignorance, impotence, impurity, vanity, and iniquity, he suffered not alone, but involved all his posterity with him, and plunged them into the same miseries. This is that hereditary corruption which the fathers called *original sin;* meaning by sin, the depravation of a nature previously good and pure; on which subject they had much contention. . . . Pelagius . . . profanely pretended, that the sin of Adam only ruined himself, and did not injure his descendants . . . , that sin . . . was communicated by imitation, not by propagation. Therefore good men, and beyond all others Augustine, have laboured to demonstrate that we are not corrupted by any adventitious means, but that we derive an innate depravity from our very birth. . . . Every descendant, therefore, from the impure source, is born infected with the contagion of sin; and even before we behold the light of life, we are in the sight of God defiled and polluted. . . . From a putrefied root . . . have sprung putrid branches, which II. i. 7 have transmitted their putrescence to remoter ramifications. For the children were so vitiated in their parent, that they became contagious to their descendants: there was in Adam such a spring of corruption, that it is transfused from parents to children in a perpetual stream. . . .

To remove all uncertainty and misunderstanding on this subject, II. i. 8 let us define original sin. It is not my intention to discuss all the definitions given by writers; I shall only produce one, which I think perfectly consistent with the truth. Original sin, therefore, appears to be an hereditary pravity and corruption of our nature, diffused through all the parts of the soul, rendering us obnoxious to the Divine wrath, and producing in us those works which the Scripture calls " works of the flesh." (*d*) . . . When it is said that the sin of Adam renders us obnoxious to the Divine judgment, it is not to be understood as if we, though innocent, were undeservedly loaded with the guilt of his sin; but, because we are all subject to a curse, in consequence of his transgression, he is therefore said to have involved us in guilt. . . . And therefore infants themselves, . . . though they have not yet produced the fruits of their iniquity, yet they have the seed of it within them; even their

---

(*d*) Gal. v. 19.

whole nature is as it were a seed of sin, and therefore cannot but
II. 1. 9　be odious and abominable to God. . . . Wherefore I have asserted
that sin has possessed all the powers of the soul. . . . Man has
not only been ensnared by the inferior appetites, but abominable
impiety has seized the very citadel of his mind, and pride has
penetrated into the inmost recesses of his heart. . . .

II. 1. 10　　Now, let us dismiss those who dare to charge God with their
corruptions, because we say that men are naturally corrupt. . . .
Our perdition . . . proceeds from the sinfulness of our flesh, not
from God. . . . And let no one murmur that God might have made
a better provision for our safety, by preventing the fall of Adam.
For such an objection ought to be abominated, as too presumptuously curious, by all pious minds. . . .

CHAPTER XI

Sin and the Freedom of the Will

❧

(1) THE WILL A SLAVE TO SIN

Man, being taught that he has nothing good left in his posses- II. ii. 1
sion, and being surrounded on every side with the·most miserable
necessity, should, nevertheless, be instructed to aspire to the good
of which he is destitute, and to the liberty of which he is deprived;
and should be roused from indolence with more earnestness, than
if he were supposed to be possessed of the greatest strength. . . .
The philosophers, indeed, with general consent, pretend, that in II. ii. 2
the mind presides Reason, which like a lamp illuminates with its
counsels, and like a queen governs the will; . . . that Sense, on
the contrary, is torpid and afflicted with weakness of sight, so that
it always creeps on the ground, and is absorbed in the grossest
objects; . . . that Appetite, if it can submit to the obedience of
reason, and resist the attractions of sense, is inclined to the practice
of virtues, travels the path of rectitude, and is formed into will;
but that, if it be devoted to the servitude of sense, it is thereby so
corrupted and depraved as to degenerate into lust. . . . They
place the will in the middle station between reason and sense, as
perfectly at liberty, whether it chooses to obey reason, or to submit to the violence of sense. . . . This, then, is the substance of II. ii. 3
the opinion of all the philosophers, that the reason of the human
understanding is sufficient for its proper government; that the
will, being subject to it, is indeed solicited by sense to evil objects,

45

but, as it has a free choice, there can be no impediment to its following reason as its guide in all things.

II. ii. 4   Among the ecclesiastical writers, though there has not been one
who would not acknowledge both that human reason is grievously
wounded by sin, and that the will is very much embarrassed by
corrupt affections, yet many of them have followed the philosophers far beyond what is right. . . . To avoid delivering any
principle deemed absurd in the common opinion of mankind, they
made it their study, therefore, to compromise between the doctrine
of the Scripture and the dogmas of the philosophers. . . . Yet
such are the variations, fluctuations, or obscurities of all the fathers, except Augustine, on this subject, that scarcely any thing
certain can be concluded from their writings. . . . Origen appears to have advanced a position to which they all assented, when
he calls it a power of *reason* to discern good and evil, of *will* to
II. ii. 5   choose either. . . . Common and external things, which do not
pertain to the kingdom of God, they generally consider as subject
to the free determination of man; but true righteousness they refer
to the special grace of God and spiritual regeneration. . . .
Hence, when writers treat of free will, their first inquiry respects
not its ability in civil or external actions, but its power to obey
the Divine law. Though I confess the latter to be the principal question, yet I think the other ought not to be wholly neglected. . . .
II. ii. 6   Man is not possessed of free will for good works, unless he be
assisted by grace, and that special grace which is bestowed on the
II. ii. 7   elect alone in regeneration. . . . Then man will be said to possess
free will in this sense, not that he has an equally free election of
good and evil, but because he does evil voluntarily, and not by
constraint. That, indeed, is very true; but what end could it answer
to decorate a thing so diminutive with a title so superb? . . .

I really abominate contentions about words, which disturb the
Church without producing any good effect; but I think that we
ought religiously to avoid words which signify any absurdity,
particularly when they lead to a pernicious error. How few are
there, pray, who, when they hear free will attributed to man, do
not immediately conceive, that he has the sovereignty over his
own mind and will, and is able by his innate power to incline him-
II. ii. 8   self to whatever he pleases? . . . Augustine, who hesitates not to

call the will a slave, . . . plainly confesses, that the human will is not free without the Spirit. . . . Having shown that free will is the result of grace, he sharply inveighs against those who arrogate it to themselves without grace. . . . Therefore, if any man allows himself the use of this term without any erroneous signification, he will not be troubled by me on that account: but because I think that it cannot be retained without great danger, and that, on the contrary, its abolition would be very beneficial to the Church, I would neither use it myself, nor wish it to be used by others who may consult my opinion.

Perhaps I may be thought to have raised a great prejudice against myself, by confessing that all the ecclesiastical writers, except Augustine, have treated this subject with such ambiguities or variations, that nothing certain can be learned from their writings. For some will interpret this, as though I intended to deprive them of the right of giving their suffrages, because their opinions are all adverse to mine. But I have had no other object in view than simply and faithfully to consult the benefit of pious minds, who, if they wait to discover the sentiments of the fathers on this subject, will fluctuate in perpetual uncertainty. . . . I have always, indeed, been exceedingly pleased with this observation of Chrysostom, that humility is the foundation of our philosophy; but still more with this of Augustine. "As a rhetorician," says he, "on being interrogated what was the first thing in the rules of eloquence, replied, 'Pronunciation'; and on being separately interrogated what was the second, and what was the third, gave the same reply; so, should any one interrogate me concerning the rules of the Christian religion, the first, second, and third, I would always reply, Humility." . . . The greater your weakness is in yourself, so much the more the Lord assists you. . . . And, indeed, I much approve of that common observation which has been borrowed from Augustine, that the natural talents in man have been corrupted by sin, but that of the supernatural ones he has been wholly deprived. . . . Reason, therefore, by which man distinguishes between good and evil, by which he understands and judges, being a natural talent, could not be totally destroyed, but is partly debilitated, partly vitiated, so that it exhibits nothing but deformity and ruin. . . . Some sparks continue to shine in the nature of

II. ii. 9

II. ii. 11

II. ii. 12

man, even in its corrupt and degenerate state, which prove him to be a rational creature, and different from the brutes, because he is endued with understanding; and yet . . . this light is smothered by so much ignorance, that it cannot act with any degree of efficacy. So the will, being inseparable from the nature of man, is not annihilated; but it is fettered by depraved and inordinate desires, so that it cannot aspire after any thing that is good. . . .

(2) THE TOTAL DEPRAVITY OF MAN

II. iii. 1   But man cannot be better known in either faculty of his soul, than when he is represented in those characters by which the Scripture has distinguished him. If he be completely described in these words of Christ, " That which is born of the flesh is flesh," (r) as it is easy to prove, it is evident that he is a very miserable creature. . . . The argument of our Lord is, that man must be born again, because he is flesh. . . . Therefore, every thing in man that is not spiritual, is, according to this mode of reasoning, denominated carnal. But we have nothing of the spirit, except by regeneration. Whatever, therefore, we have from nature is carnal. . . .

II. iii. 2   Equally severe is the condemnation of the heart, when it is called " deceitful above all things, and desperately wicked." (y) . . . The Apostle, when he wishes to demolish the arrogance of mankind, does it by these testimonies: " There is none righteous, no, not one." . . . He does not declaim against the depraved manners of one or another age, but accuses the perpetual corruption of our nature. For his design in that passage is not simply to rebuke men, in order that they may repent, but rather to teach us that all men are overwhelmed with an inevitable calamity, from which they can never emerge unless they are extricated by the mercy of God. . . .

II. iii. 3   A question, nearly the same as we have already answered, here presents itself to us again. For in all ages there have been some persons, who, from the mere dictates of nature, have devoted their whole lives to the pursuit of virtue. And though many errors might perhaps be discovered in their conduct, yet by their pursuit of

---

(r) John iii. 6.   (y) Jer. xvii. 9.

virtue they afforded a proof, that there was some degree of purity in their nature. . . . These examples . . . seem to teach us that we should not consider human nature to be totally corrupted; since, from its instinctive bias, some men have not only been eminent for noble actions, but have uniformly conducted themselves in a most virtuous manner through the whole course of their lives. But here we ought to remember, that amidst this corruption of nature there is some room for Divine grace, not to purify it, but internally to restrain its operations. For should the Lord permit the minds of all men to give up the reins to every lawless passion, there certainly would not be an individual in the world, whose actions would not evince all the crimes, for which Paul condemns human nature in general, to be most truly applicable to him. For can you except yourself from the number of those whose feet are swift to shed blood, whose hands are polluted with rapine and murder, whose throats are like open sepulchres, whose tongues are deceitful, whose lips are envenomed, whose works are useless, iniquitous, corrupt, and deadly, whose souls are estranged from God, the inmost recesses of whose hearts are full of pravity, whose eyes are insidiously employed, whose minds are elated with insolence — in a word, all whose powers are prepared for the commission of atrocious and innumerable crimes? If every soul be subject to all these monstrous vices, as the Apostle fearlessly pronounces, we clearly see what would be the consequence, if the Lord should suffer the human passions to go all the lengths, to which they are inclined. . . . Thus God by his providence restrains the perverseness of our nature from breaking out into external acts, but does not purify it within. . . .

The will, therefore, is so bound by the slavery of sin, that it **II. iii. 5** cannot excite itself, much less devote itself to any thing good. . . . We must . . . observe this grand point of distinction, that man, having been corrupted by his fall, sins voluntarily, not with reluctance or constraint; with the strongest propensity of disposition, not with violent coercion; with the bias of his own passions, and not with external compulsion: yet such is the pravity of his nature, that he cannot be excited and biassed to any thing but what is evil. If this be true, there is no impropriety in affirming, that he is under a necessity of sinning. . . .

(3) WHAT GOOD THERE IS IN MAN DUE TO THE GRACE OF GOD

II. iii. 6   It is necessary, on the other hand, to consider the remedy of Divine grace, by which the depravity of nature is corrected and healed. . . . God begins the good work in us by exciting in our hearts a love, desire, and ardent pursuit of righteousness; or, to speak more properly, by bending, forming, and directing our hearts towards righteousness; but he completes it, by confirming us to perseverance. . . . If there be in a stone any softness, which, by some application, being made more tender, would be flexible in every direction, then I will not deny the flexibility of the human heart to the obedience of rectitude, provided its imperfections are supplied by the grace of God. . . . If, therefore, when God converts us to the pursuit of rectitude, this change is like the transformation of a stone into flesh, it follows, that whatever belongs to our own will is removed, and what succeeds to it is entirely from God. The will, I say, is removed, not considered as the will; because, in the conversion of man, the properties of our original nature remain entire. I assert also, that it is created anew, not that the will then begins to exist, but that it is then converted from an evil into a good one. . . . Whatever good is in the human will, is the work of pure grace. . . .

II. iii. 7   But there may be some, who will concede that the will, being, of its own spontaneous inclination, averse to what is good, is converted solely by the power of the Lord; yet in such a manner, that being previously prepared, it has also its own share in the work; that grace, as Augustine teaches, precedes every good work, the will following grace, not leading it, being its companion, not its guide. . . . As it is preceded by grace, I allow you to style it an attendant; but since its reformation is the work of the Lord, it is wrong to attribute to man a voluntary obedience in following the guidance of grace. . . . Nor was it the intention of Augustine, when he called the human will the companion of grace, to assign to it any secondary office next to grace in the good work; but with a view to refute the nefarious dogma broached by Pelagius, who made the prime cause of salvation to consist in human merit, he contends, what was sufficient for his present argument, that grace

is prior to all merit. . . . The origin of all good clearly appears,   II. iii. 8
from a plain and certain reason, to be from no other than from
God alone; for no propensity of the will to any thing good can
be found but in the elect. But the cause of election must not be
sought in men. Whence we may conclude, that man has not a good
will from himself, but that it proceeds from the same decree by
which we were elected before the creation of the world. . . .

Concerning perseverance there would have been no doubt that   II. iii. 11
it ought to be esteemed the gratuitous gift of God, had it not been
for the prevalence of a pestilent error, that it is dispensed according to the merit of men, in proportion to the gratitude which each
person has discovered for the grace bestowed on him. But as that
opinion arose from the supposition that it was at our own option
to reject or accept the offered grace of God, this notion being ex-
ploded, the other falls of course. . . . But here two errors must
be avoided; the legitimate use of the grace first bestowed must not
be said to be rewarded with subsequent degrees of grace, as though
man, by his own industry, rendered the grace of God efficacious;
nor must it be accounted a remuneration in such a sense as to cease
to be esteemed the free favour of God. . . .

(4) THE WILL OF MAN IS NOT FREE

Man is so enslaved by sin, as to be of his own nature incapable   II. iv. 1
of an effort, or even an inspiration, towards that which is good.
. . . Augustine somewhere compares the human will to a horse,
obedient to the direction of his rider; and God and the devil he
compares to riders. " If God rides it, he, like a sober and skilful
rider, manages it in a graceful manner; stimulates its tardiness;
restrains its immoderate celerity; represses its wantonness and
wildness; tames its perverseness, and conducts it into the right
way. But if the devil has taken possession of it, he, like a foolish
and wanton rider, forces it through pathless places, hurries it into
ditches, drives it down over precipices, and excites it to obstinacy
and ferocity." . . .

Those whom the Lord does not favour with the government of
his Spirit, he abandons, in righteous judgment, to the influence of
Satan. . . . The blinding of the wicked, and all those enormities

which attend it, are called the works of Satan, the cause of which must nevertheless be sought only in the human will, from which proceeds the root of evil, and in which rests the foundation of the kingdom of Satan, that is, sin. . . . The fathers are sometimes too scrupulous on this subject, and afraid of a simple confession of the truth, lest they should afford an occasion to impiety to speak irreverently and reproachfully of the works of God. Though I highly approve this sobriety, yet I think we are in no danger, if we simply maintain what the Scripture delivers. . . . God is very frequently said to blind and harden the reprobate, and to turn, incline, and influence their hearts. . . .

II. iv. 3

II. iv. 6

What liberty man possesses in those actions which in themselves are neither righteous nor wicked, and pertain rather to the corporeal than to the spiritual life . . . has not yet been explicitly stated. Some have admitted him in such things to possess a free choice. . . . But I maintain . . . that God, whenever he designs to prepare the way for his providence, inclines and moves the wills of men even in external things, and that their choice is not so free, but that its liberty is subject to the will of God. That your mind depends more on the influence of God, than on the liberty of your own choice, you must be constrained to conclude, whether you are willing or not, from this daily experience, that in affairs of no perplexity your judgment and understanding frequently fail; that in undertakings not arduous your spirits languish; on the other hand, in things the most obscure, suitable advice is immediately offered; in things great and perilous, your mind proves superior to every difficulty. . . . In the dispute concerning free will, the question is not, whether a man, notwithstanding external impediments, can perform and execute whatever he may have resolved in his mind, but whether in every case his judgment exerts freedom of choice, and his will freedom of inclination. . . .

II. iv. 7

II. iv. 8

(5) REFUTATION OF OBJECTIONS URGED IN SUPPORT OF FREE WILL

II. v. 1

They, who endeavour to overthrow [the servitude of the human will] . . . with a false notion of liberty, allege . . . to render it odious, as if it were abhorrent to common sense; and then they attack it with testimonies of Scripture. . . . If sin, say they, be necessary, then it ceases to be sin; if it be voluntary, then it may be avoided. . . . I deny . . . that sin is the less criminal, because it is necessary; I deny also the other consequence, which they infer, that it is avoidable because it is voluntary. For, if any one wish to dispute with God, and to escape his judgment by the pretext of having been incapable of acting otherwise, he is prepared with an answer, which we have elsewhere advanced, that it arises not from creation, but from the corruption of nature, that men, being enslaved by sin, can will nothing but what is evil. . . . The corruption with which we are firmly bound . . . originated in the revolt of the first man from his Maker. If all men are justly accounted guilty of this rebellion, let them not suppose themselves excused by necessity. . . . The second branch of their argument is erroneous; because it makes an improper transition from what is voluntary to what is free. . . .

They add, that unless both virtues and vices proceed from the free choice of the will, it is not reasonable either that punishments should be inflicted, or that rewards should be conferred on man. . . . In regard to punishments, I reply, that they are justly inflicted on us, from whom the guilt of sin proceeds. For of what importance is it, whether sin be committed with a judgment free or enslaved, so it be committed with the voluntary bias of the passions . . . ? With respect to rewards of righteousness, where is the great absurdity, if we confess that they depend rather on the Divine benignity than on our own merits? . . . II. v. 2

They further allege . . . that if our will has not this ability to choose good or evil, the partakers of the same nature must be either all evil or all good. . . . It is the election of God, which makes this difference between men. We are not afraid to allow, what Paul very strenuously asserts, that all, without exception, are depraved and addicted to wickedness; but with him we add, that the mercy of God does not permit all to remain in depravity. Therefore, since we all naturally labour under the same disease, they alone recover to whom the Lord has been pleased to apply his healing hand. The rest, whom he passes by in righteous judgment, putrefy in their corruption till they are entirely consumed. . . . II. v. 3

They urge further, that exhortations are given in vain, that the II.

use of admonitions is superfluous, and that reproofs are ridiculous, if it be not in the power of the sinner to obey. . . . . God does not regulate the precepts of his law by the ability of men, but when he has commanded what is right, freely gives to his elect ability to perform it. . . . We are not alone in this cause, but have the support of Christ and all the Apostles. . . . Does Christ, who declares that without him we can do nothing, (o) on that account the less reprehend and punish those who without him do what is

II. v. 5 evil? . . . The operations of God on his elect are twofold — internally, by his Spirit, externally, by his word. By his Spirit illuminating their minds and forming their hearts to the love and cultivation of righteousness, he makes them new creatures. By his word he excites them to desire, seek, and obtain the same renovation. In both he displays the efficacy of his power. . . . When he addresses the same word to the reprobate, though it produces not their correction, yet he makes it effectual for another purpose, that they may be confounded by the testimony of their consciences now, and be rendered more inexcusable at the day of judgment. . . .

II. v. 6 Our adversaries are very laborious in collecting testimonies of Scripture; and this with a view, since they cannot refute us with their weight, to overwhelm us with their number. . . . Either, say they, God mocks us, when he commands holiness, piety, obedience, chastity, love, and meekness, and when he forbids impurity, idolatry, unchastity, anger, robbery, pride, and the like; or he requires only such things as we have power to perform. Now, almost all the precepts which they collect, may be distributed into three classes. Some require the first conversion to God; others simply relate to the observation of the law; others enjoin perseverance in the grace of God already received. . . .

II. v. 9 Our more subtle adversaries cavil . . . because there is no impediment, they say, that prevents our exerting our own ability, and God assisting our weak efforts. They adduce . . . passages from the Prophets, where the accomplishment of our conversion seems to be divided equally between God and us. "Turn ye unto me, and I will turn unto you." (i) . . . I wish only this single

---

(o) John xv. 5.   (i) Zech. i. 3.

point to be conceded to me, that it is in vain to infer our possession of ability to fulfil the law from God's command to us to obey it; since it is evident, that for the performance of all the Divine precepts, the grace of the Legislator is both necessary for us, and promised to us; and hence it follows, that at least more is required of us than we are capable of performing. . . .

The second description of arguments is nearly allied to the **II. v. 10** first. They allege the promises, in which God covenants with our will; such as, " Seek good, and not evil, that ye may live." " If ye be willing and obedient, ye shall eat the good of the land; but if ye refuse and rebel, ye shall be devoured with the sword; for the mouth of the Lord hath spoken it." (*l*) . . . They consider it an absurdity and mockery, that the benefits which the Lord offers in the promises are referred to our will, unless it be in our power either to confirm or to frustrate them. . . . I deny that God is cruel or insincere to us, when he invites us to merit his favours, though he knows us to be altogether incapable of doing this. For as the promises are offered equally to the faithful and to the impious, they have their use with them both. As by the precepts God disturbs the consciences of the impious, that they may not enjoy too much pleasure in sin without any recollection of his judgments, so in the promises he calls them to attest how unworthy they are of his kindness. For who can deny that it is most equitable and proper for the Lord to bless those who worship him, and severely to punish the despisers of his majesty? God acts, therefore, in a right and orderly manner, when, addressing the impious, who are bound with the fetters of sin, he adds to the promises this condition, that when they shall have departed from their wickedness, they shall then, and not till then, enjoy his favours; even for this sole reason, that they may know that they are deservedly excluded from those benefits which belong to the worshippers of the true God. . . .

The third class of arguments also has a great affinity with the **II. v. 11** preceding. For they produce passages in which God reproaches an ungrateful people, that it was wholly owing to their own fault that they did not receive blessings of all kinds from his indulgent

---

(*l*) Amos v. 14.   Isaiah i. 19, 20.

hand. Of this kind are the following passages: "The Amalekites and the Canaanites are there before you, and ye shall fall by the sword; because ye are turned away from the Lord." (n) " Because I called you, but ye answered not, therefore will I do unto this house as I have done to Shiloh." (o) . . . How, say they, could such reproaches be applicable to those who might immediately reply, It is true that we desired prosperity and dreaded adversity; but our not obeying the Lord, or hearkening to his voice, in order to obtain good and to avoid evil, has been owing to our want of liberty, and subjection to the dominion of sin. It is in vain, therefore, to reproach us with evils, which we had no power to avoid. . . . I ask whether they can exculpate themselves from all guilt. For if they are convicted of any fault, the Lord justly reproaches them with their perverseness, as the cause of their not having experienced the advantage of his clemency. Let them answer, then, if they can deny that their own perverse will was the cause of their obstinacy. If they find the source of the evil within themselves, why do they so earnestly inquire after extraneous causes, that they may not appear to have been the authors of their own ruin? . . .

II. v. 19   Let us hold this, then, as an undoubted truth, which no opposition can ever shake — that the mind of man is so completely alienated from the righteousness of God, that it conceives, desires, and undertakes every thing that is impious, perverse, base, impure, and flagitious; that his heart is so thoroughly infected by the poison of sin, that it cannot produce any thing but what is corrupt; and that if at any time men do any thing apparently good, yet the mind always remains involved in hypocrisy and fallacious obliquity, and the heart enslaved by its inward perverseness. . . .

(n) Numb. xiv. 43.   (o) Jer. vii. 13, 14.

CHAPTER XII

Sin and the Law of God

(1) MAN'S INABILITY TO KEEP THE LAW

BY THE word *law*, I intend, not only the decalogue, which prescribes the rule of a pious and righteous life, but the form of religion delivered from God by the hands of Moses. For Moses was not made a legislator to abolish the blessing promised to the seed of Abraham; on the contrary, we see him on every occasion reminding the Jews of that gracious covenant made with their fathers, to which they were heirs; as though the object of his mission had been to renew it. It was very clearly manifested in the ceremonies. For what could be more vain or frivolous than for men to offer the fetid stench arising from the fat of cattle, in order to reconcile themselves to God? or to resort to any aspersion of water or of blood, to cleanse themselves from pollution? In short, the whole legal worship, if it be considered in itself, and contain no shadows and figures of correspondent truths, will appear perfectly ridiculous. Wherefore it is not without reason, that both in the speech of Stephen and in the Epistle to the Hebrews, that passage is so carefully stated, in which God commands Moses to make all things pertaining to the tabernacle " according to the pattern showed to him in the mount." (*m*) For unless there had

---

(*m*) Acts vii. 44. Heb. viii. 5. Ex. xxv. 40.

been some spiritual design, to which they were directed, the Jews would have laboured to no purpose in these observances, as the Gentiles did in their mummeries. Profane men, who have never seriously devoted themselves to the pursuit of piety, have not patience to hear of such various rites: they not only wonder why God should weary his ancient people with such a mass of cere- monies, but they even despise and deride them as puerile and ludi- crous. This arises from inattention to the end of the legal figures, from which if those figures be separated, they must be condemned as vain and useless. But the " pattern," which is mentioned, shows that God commanded the sacrifices, not with a design to occupy his worshippers in terrestrial exercises, but rather that he might elevate their minds to sublimer objects. . . .

II. vii. 2   The author of the Epistle to the Hebrews, from the fourth chap- ter to the eleventh, demonstrates in a manner sufficiently copious and clear, that, irrespective of Christ, all the ceremonies of the law are worthless and vain. And in regard to the decalogue, we should attend to the declaration of Paul, that " Christ is the end of the law for righteousness to every one that believeth; " (t) and also that Christ is " the Spirit," who gives " life " to the otherwise dead letter. (v) For in the former passage he signifies that right- eousness is taught in vain by the precepts, till Christ bestows it both by a gratuitous imputation, and by the Spirit of regenera- tion. Wherefore he justly denominates Christ the completion or end of the law; for we should derive no benefit from a knowledge of what God requires of us, unless we were succoured by Christ when labouring and oppressed under its yoke and intolerable bur- den. In another place, he states that " the law was added because of transgressions; " (w) that is, to humble men, by convicting them of being the causes of their own condemnation. Now, this being the true and only preparation for seeking Christ, the vari- ous declarations which he makes are in perfect unison with each other. . . .

II. vii. 3   If it be true that the law displays a perfection of righteousness, it also follows that the complete observation of it, is in the sight of God a perfect righteousness, in which a man would be esteemed

---

(t) Rom. x. 4.   (v) 2 Cor. iii. 17.   (w) Gal. iii. 19.

and reputed righteous at the tribunal of heaven. . . . But, on
the other hand, it is proper to examine whether we perform that
obedience, the merit of which can warrant our confident expectation of that reward. For how unimportant is it, to discover that
the reward of eternal life depends on the observance of the law,
unless we also ascertain whether it be possible for us to arrive
at eternal life in that way! . . . If we direct our views exclusively   II. vii. 4
to the law, the effects upon our minds will only be despondency,
confusion, and despair, since it condemns and curses us all, and
keeps us far from that blessedness which it proposes to them who
observe it. . . .

The Apostle indeed declares that we are all condemned by the   II. vii. 8
sentence of the law, " that every mouth may be stopped, and all
the world may become guilty before God." (*l*) Yet the same
Apostle elsewhere informs us, that " God hath concluded them
all in unbelief," not that he might destroy or suffer all to perish,
but " that he might have mercy upon all; " (*m*) that is, that leaving their foolish opinion of their own strength, they may know
that they stand and are supported only by the power of God;
that being naked and destitute, they may resort for assistance to
his mercy, recline themselves wholly upon it, hide themselves
entirely in it, and embrace it alone for righteousness and merits,
since it is offered in Christ to all who with true faith implore it
and expect it. For in the precepts of the law, God appears only,
on the one hand, as the rewarder of perfect righteousness, of
which we are all destitute; and on the other, as the severe judge
of transgressions. But in Christ, his face shines with a plenitude of
grace and lenity, even towards miserable and unworthy sinners. . . .

(2) EXPOSITION OF THE MORAL LAW

Here I think it will not be foreign to our subject to introduce   II. viii. 1
the ten precepts of the law, with a brief exposition of them. For
this will more clearly evince what I have suggested, that the service
which God has once prescribed always remains in full force; and

---

(*l*) Rom. iii. 19.   (*m*) Rom. xi. 32.

will also furnish us with a confirmation of the second remark, that the Jews not only learned from it the nature of true piety, but when they saw their inability to observe it, were led by the fear of its sentence, though not without reluctance, to the Mediator. Now, in giving a summary of those things which are requisite to the true knowledge of God, we have shown that we can form no conceptions of his greatness, but his majesty immediately discovers itself to us, to constrain us to worship him. In the knowledge of ourselves, we have laid down this as a principal article, that being divested of all opinion of our own strength, and confidence in our own righteousness, and, on the other hand, discouraged and depressed by a consciousness of our poverty, we should learn true humility and self-dejection. The Lord accomplishes both these things in his law, where, in the first place, claiming to himself the legitimate authority to command, he calls us to revere his Divinity, and prescribes the parts of which this reverence consists; and in the next place, promulgating the rule of his righteousness, (the rectitude of which, our nature, being depraved and perverted, perpetually opposes; and from the perfection of which, our ability, through its indolence and imbecility towards that which is good, is at a great distance,) he convicts us both of impotence and of unrighteousness. Moreover, the internal law, which has before been said to be inscribed and as it were engraven on the hearts of all men, suggests to us in some measure the same things which are to be learned from the two tables. For our conscience does not permit us to sleep in perpetual insensibility, but is an internal witness and monitor of the duties we owe to God, shows us the difference between good and evil, and so accuses us when we deviate from our duty. But man, involved as he is in a cloud of errors, scarcely obtains from this law of nature the smallest idea of what worship is accepted by God; but is certainly at an immense distance from a right understanding of it. Besides, he is so elated with arrogance and ambition, and so blinded with self-love, that he cannot yet take a view of himself, and as it were retire within, that he may learn to submit and humble himself, and to confess his misery. Since it was necessary, therefore, both for our dulness and obstinacy, the Lord gave us a written law; to declare with greater certainty what in the law of nature was too obscure, and by arousing our indolence, to make a deeper impression on our understanding and memory.

Now, it is easy to perceive, what we are to learn from the law; namely, that God, as he is our Creator, justly sustains towards us the character of a Father and of a Lord; and that on this account we owe to him glory and reverence, love and fear. . . . II. viii. 2

By comparing our life with the righteousness of the law, we shall find, that we are very far from acting agreeably to the will of God. . . . By examining our strength, we shall see, that it is not only unequal to the observance of the law, but a mere nullity. The necessary consequence of this will be a diffidence in our own strength, and an anxiety and trepidation of mind. . . . The result of all this is, that the man terrified with the apprehension of eternal death, which he sees justly impending over him for his unrighteousness, betakes himself entirely to the Divine mercy, as to the only port of salvation; and perceiving his inability to fulfil the commands of the law. and feeling nothing but despair in himself, he implores and expects assistance from another quarter. . . . II. viii. 3

Before we enter, however, on the discussion of each article separately, it will be useful to premise some things which may contribute to a general knowledge of it. First, let it be understood, that the law inculcates a conformity of life, not only to external probity, but also to internal and spiritual righteousness. . . . The superintendence of a mortal legislator extends only to the external conduct, and his prohibitions are not violated unless the crimes be actually committed. But God, whose eye nothing escapes, and who esteems not so much the external appearance as the purity of the heart, in the prohibition of adultery, murder, and theft, comprises a prohibition of lust, wrath, hatred, coveting what belongs to another, fraud, and every similar vice. For, being a spiritual Legislator, he addresses himself to the soul as much as to the body. Now, the murder of the soul is wrath and hatred; the theft of the soul is evil concupiscence and avarice; the adultery of the soul is lust. . . . Human laws therefore are satisfied, when a man abstains from external transgression. But, on the contrary, the Divine law being given to our minds, the proper regulation of them is the principal requisite to a righteous observance of it. . . . When we say that this is the sense of the law, we are not introducing a novel II. viii. 6

II. viii. 7

interpretation of our own, but following Christ, who is the best interpreter of it. . . . He . . . pronounces an unchaste look at a woman to be adultery; he declares them to be murderers, who hate a brother; he makes them " in danger of the judgment," who have only conceived resentment in their hearts; them " in danger of the council," who in murmuring or quarrelling have discovered any sign of an angry mind; and them " in danger of hell fire," who with opprobrious and slanderous language have broken forth into open rage. (*m*) . . .

II. viii. 8   It must be observed, in the second place, that the commands and prohibitions always imply more than the words express. . . . A sober exposition of the law goes beyond the words of it; but how far, remains doubtful, unless some rule be laid down. The best rule, then, I conceive will be, that the exposition be directed to the design of the precept; that in regard to every precept it should

II. viii. 9   be considered for what end it was given. . . . In this precept, " Thou shalt not kill," the common sense of mankind will perceive nothing more than that we ought to abstain from all acts of injury to others, and from all desire to commit any such acts. I maintain that it also implies, that we should do every thing that we possibly can towards the preservation of the life of our neighbour. . . .

II. viii. 11   In the third place, let it be considered, what is intended by the division of the Divine law into two tables. . . . God has divided his law into two parts, which comprise the perfection of righteousness, so that he has assigned the first part to the duties of religion, which peculiarly belongs to the worship of his majesty, and the second to those duties of charity, which respect men. . . . It is in vain . . . to boast of righteousness without religion; as well might the trunk of a body be exhibited as a beautiful object, after the head has been cut off. Nor is religion only the head of righteousness, but the very soul of it, constituting all its life and vigour; for without the fear of God, men preserve no equity and love among themselves. . . .

II. viii. 12   Now let us hear God himself speaking in his own words.

(*m*) Matt. v. 22, 28.

THE FIRST COMMANDMENT

I am the Lord thy God, which have brought thee out of the land   II. viii. 13
of Egypt, out of the house of bondage. Thou shalt have no other
gods before me.

Whether you make the first sentence a part of the first commandment, or read it separately, is a matter of indifference to me,
provided you allow it to be a preface to the whole law. . . . God
in the first place provides, that the majesty of the law, which he
is about to deliver, may never fall into contempt. . . . He asserts
his authority and right of giving commands, and thereby lays his
chosen people under a necessity of obeying them. He exhibits a
promise of grace, to allure them by its charms to the pursuit of
holiness. He reminds the Israelites of his favour, to convict them
of ingratitude if they do not conduct themselves in a manner
correspondent to his goodness. . . . Having firmly established   II. viii. 16
the authority of his law, he publishes the first commandment,
" That we should have no other gods before him." . . . For he requires from us the glory due to his Divinity undiminished and un-
corrupted, not only in external confession, but in his own eyes,
which penetrate the inmost recesses of our hearts.

THE SECOND COMMANDMENT

Thou shalt not make unto thee any graven image, or any like-   II. viii. 17
ness of any thing that is in heaven above, or that is in the earth
beneath, or that is in the water under the earth. Thou shalt
not bow down thyself to them, nor serve them.

. . . The end . . . of this precept is, that he will not have his
legitimate worship profaned with superstitious rites. . . . The   II. viii. 18
penal sanction which is annexed ought to have no small influence
in arousing us from our lethargy. He thus threatens:

For I the Lord thy God am a jealous God, visiting the iniquity
of the fathers upon the children unto the third and fourth
generation of them that hate me; and showing mercy unto
thousands of them that love me, and keep my commandments.

This is equivalent to a declaration that it is to him alone that we ought to adhere. And to urge us to it, he announces his power, which he permits none with impunity to despise or undervalue.

II. viii. 19 . . . Let us inquire what he intends by his threatening to "visit the iniquity of the fathers upon the children to the third and fourth generation." For besides that it is inconsistent with the equity of the Divine justice to inflict upon an innocent person the punishment due to the offences of another, God himself declares that "the son shall not bear the iniquity of the father." (z) . . . Some, who labour very hard to solve this difficulty, are of opinion that its meaning is to be confined to temporal punishments. . . . But when this is adduced as a solution of these questions, it is rather an evasion of it, than a proper explanation. For in this and in similar places the Lord threatens a punishment too great to be terminated by the limits of the present life. It must therefore be understood as a declaration that the curse of the Lord righteously rests, not only on the person of an impious man, but also on his whole family. Where it has rested, what can be expected, but that the father, being destitute of the Spirit of God, will lead a most flagitious life; and that the son, experiencing, in consequence of the iniquity of his father, a similar dereliction by the Lord, will pursue the same path to perdition; and that the grandson and the great grandson, the execrable posterity of detestable men, will run headlong after them down the same precipice of destruction? . . .

THE THIRD COMMANDMENT

Thou shalt not take the name of the Lord thy God in vain.

II. viii. 22   The end of this precept is, that the Lord will have the majesty of his name to be held inviolably sacred by us. The substance of the command therefore is that we ought not profane that name by a contemptuous or irreverent use of it. . . . These three things, I say, we ought most carefully to observe — first, that whatever we think, and whatever we say of him, should savour of his excellence, correspond to the sacred sublimity of his name, and tend to the exaltation of his magnificence. Secondly, we should not rashly and

---

(z) Ezek. xviii. 20.

preposterously abuse his holy word and adorable mysteries to the purposes of ambition, of avarice, or of amusement; but as they bear an impression of the dignity of his name, they should always receive from us the honour and esteem which belong to them. Lastly, we should not injure his works by obloquy or detraction, as some miserable mortals are accustomed to do; but whenever we mention any thing done by him, we should celebrate it with encomiums of wisdom, justice, and goodness. This is " sanctifying " the name of God. . . . In the first place, we have to explain what an oath is. It consists in calling upon God to witness, to confirm the truth of any declaration that we make. . . . It is no trifling insult to him, when perjury is committed in his name; and therefore the law calls it a profanation. (n) But what remains to the Lord, when he is despoiled of his truth? he will then cease to be God. But he is certainly despoiled of it, when he is made an abettor and approver of a falsehood. . . . I can find . . . no better rule, than that we regulate our oaths in such a manner, that they be not rash or inconsiderate, wanton or frivolous, but used in cases of real necessity, as for vindicating the glory of the Lord, or promoting the edification of our brother; which is the end of this commandment of the law.

II. viii. 23

II. viii. 24

II. viii. 27

THE FOURTH COMMANDMENT

Remember the sabbath day, to keep it holy. Six days shalt thou labour, and do all thy work; but the seventh day is the sabbath of the Lord thy God; in it thou shalt not do any work, &c.

· The end of this precept is, that, being dead to our own affections and works, we should meditate on the kingdom of God, and be exercised in that meditation in the observance of his institutions. . . . The fathers frequently call it a *shadowy commandment*, because it contains the external observance of the day, which was abolished with the rest of the figures at the advent of Christ. And there is much truth in their observation; but it reaches only half of the subject. Wherefore it is necessary to seek further for an exposition, and to consider three causes, on which I think I

II. viii. 28

(n) Lev. xix. 12.

have observed this commandment to rest. For it was the design of the heavenly Lawgiver, under the rest of the seventh day, to give the people of Israel a figure of the spiritual rest, by which the faithful ought to refrain from their own works, in order to leave God to work within them. His design was, secondly, that there should be a stated day, on which they might assemble together to hear the law and perform the ceremonies, or at least which they might especially devote to meditations on his works; that by this recollection they might be led to the exercises of piety. Thirdly, he thought it right that servants, and persons living under the jurisdiction of others, should be indulged with a day of rest,

II. viii. 29   that they might enjoy some remission from their labour. . . . We must rest altogether, that God may operate within us; we must recede from our own will, resign our own heart, and renounce all our carnal affections; in short, we must cease from all the efforts of our own understanding, that having God operating within us, we may enjoy rest in him, as we are also taught by the

II. viii. 31   Apostle. (l) . . . But all that is contained of a ceremonial nature was without doubt abolished by the advent of the Lord Christ. For he is the truth, at whose presence all figures disappear; the body, at the sight of which all the shadows are relinquished. He, I say, is the true fulfilment of the sabbath. . . . This is contained not in one day, but in the whole course of our life, till, being wholly dead to ourselves, we be filled with the life of God. Christians therefore ought to depart from all superstitious observance of days. . . .

II. viii. 33   In the present age, some unquiet spirits have been raising noisy contentions respecting the Lord's day. . . . We celebrate it not
·   with scrupulous rigour, as a ceremony which we conceive to be a figure of some spiritual mystery, but only use it as a remedy neces-

II. viii. 34   sary to the preservation of order in the Church. . . . However, the ancients have not without sufficient reason substituted what we call the Lord's day in the room of the sabbath. For since the resurrection of the Lord is the end and consummation of that true rest, which was adumbrated by the ancient sabbath, the same day which put an end to the shadows, admonishes Christians not to

---

(l) Heb. iv. 9.

adhere to a shadowy ceremony. Yet I do not lay so much stress on the septenary number, that I would oblige the Church to an invariable adherence to it; nor will I condemn those churches which have other solemn days for their assemblies, provided they keep at a distance from superstition. . . . The principal thing to be remembered is the general doctrine; that, lest religion decay or languish among us, sacred assemblies ought diligently to be held, and that we ought to use those external means which are adapted to support the worship of God.

THE FIFTH COMMANDMENT

Honour thy father and thy mother; that thy days may be long upon the land which the Lord thy God giveth thee.

The end of this precept is, that since the Lord God desires the preservation of the order he has appointed, the degrees of preeminence fixed by him ought to be inviolably preserved. The sum of it, therefore, will be, that we should reverence them whom God has exalted to any authority over us, and should render them honour, obedience, and gratitude. . . . Wherefore it ought not to be doubted that God here lays down a universal rule for our conduct; namely, that to every one, whom we know to be placed in authority over us by his appointment, we should render reverence, obedience, gratitude, and all the other services in our power. Nor does it make any difference, whether they are worthy of this honour, or not. For whatever be their characters, yet it is not without the appointment of the Divine providence, that they have attained that station, on account of which the supreme Legislator has commanded them to be honoured. . . .

II. viii. 35

II. viii. 36

THE SIXTH COMMANDMENT

Thou shalt not kill.

The end of this precept is, that since God has connected mankind together in a kind of unity, every man ought to consider himself as charged with the safety of all. . . . And therefore we are enjoined, if it be in our power, to assist in protecting the

II. viii. 39

lives of our neighbours; to exert ourselves with fidelity for this purpose; to procure those things which conduce to their tranquillity; to be vigilant in shielding them from injuries; and in cases of danger to afford them our assistance. . . . Mental homicide . . . is likewise prohibited, and an internal disposition to preserve the life of our brother is commanded in this law. The hand, indeed, accomplishes the homicide, but it is conceived by the

II. viii. 40 mind under the influence of anger and hatred. . . . That person, therefore, is not innocent of the crime of murder, who has merely restrained himself from the effusion of blood. If you perpetrate, if you attempt, if you only conceive in your mind any thing inimical to the safety of another, you stand guilty of murder. Unless you also endeavour to defend him to the utmost of your ability and opportunity, you are guilty of the same inhuman transgression of the law. But if so much concern be discovered for the safety of the body, we may conclude, how much care and attention should be devoted to the safety of the soul, which, in the sight of God, is of infinitely superior value.

THE SEVENTH COMMANDMENT

Thou shalt not commit adultery.

II. viii. 41   The end of this precept is, that because God loves chastity and purity, we ought to depart from all uncleanness. The sum of it therefore is, that we ought not to be polluted by any carnal impurity, or libidinous intemperance. . . . Every other union, but that of marriage, is cursed in his sight; and . . . the conjugal union itself is appointed as a remedy for our necessity, that we

II. viii. 44 may not break out into unrestrained licentiousness. . . . If we aspire to obedience, neither let our mind internally burn with depraved concupiscence, nor let our eyes wanton into corrupt affections, nor let our body be adorned for purposes of seduction, nor let our tongue with impure speeches allure our mind to similar thoughts, nor let us inflame ourselves with intemperance. For all these vices are stains, by which the purity of chastity is defiled.

THE EIGHTH COMMANDMENT

Thou shalt not steal.

The end of this precept is, that, as injustice is an abomination to God, every man may possess what belongs to him. The sum of it, then, is, that we are forbidden to covet the property of others, and are therefore enjoined faithfully to use our endeavours to preserve to every man what justly belongs to him. . . . God . . . sees the cruel and inhuman laws, by which the more powerful man oppresses and ruins him that is weaker. He sees the baits with which the more crafty trepan the imprudent. All which things are concealed from the judgment of man, nor ever come to his knowledge. And this kind of injury relates not only to money, or to goods, or to lands, but to whatever each individual is justly entitled to; for we defraud our neighbours of their property, if we deny them those kind offices, which it is our duty to perform to them. . . . **II. viii. 45**

We shall rightly obey this commandment therefore, if, contented with our own lot, we seek no gain but in an honest and lawful way; if we neither desire to enrich ourselves by injustice, nor attempt to ruin the fortune of our neighbour, in order to increase our own; if we do not labour to accumulate wealth by cruelty, and at the expense of the blood of others; if we do not greedily scrape together from every quarter, regardless of right or wrong, whatever may conduce to satiate our avarice or support our prodigality. On the contrary, it should be our constant aim, as far as possible, faithfully to assist all by our advice and our property in preserving what belongs to them; but if we are concerned with perfidious and fallacious men, let us be prepared rather to recede a little from our just right than to contend with them. Moreover, let us communicate to the necessities, and according to our ability alleviate the poverty, of those whom we perceive to be pressed by any embarrassment of their circumstances. Lastly, let every man examine what obligations his duty lays him under to others, and let him faithfully discharge the duties which he owes them. For this reason the people should honour their governors, patiently submit to their authority, obey **II. viii. 46** their laws and mandates, and resist nothing, to which they can submit consistently with the Divine will. On the other hand, let governors take care of their people, preserve the public peace, protect the good, punish the wicked, and administer all things in such a manner, as becomes those who must render an account of their office to God the supreme Judge. Let the ministers of churches faithfully devote themselves to the ministry of the word, and let them never adulterate the doctrine of salvation, but deliver it pure and uncontaminated to the people of God. Let them teach, not only by their doctrine, but by the example of their lives; in a word, let them preside as good shepherds over the sheep. Let the people, on their part, receive them as the messengers and apostles of God, render to them that honour to which the supreme Master has exalted them, and furnish them with the necessaries of life. Let parents undertake the support, government, and instruction of their children, as committed by God to their care; nor let them exasperate their minds and alienate their affections from them by cruelty, but cherish and embrace them with the lenity and indulgence becoming their character. And that obedience is due to them from their children has been before observed. Let juniors revere old age, since the Lord has designed that age to be honourable. Let old men, by their prudence and superior experience, guide the imbecility of youth; not teasing them with sharp and clamorous invectives, but tempering severity with mildness and affability. Let servants show themselves obedient and diligent in the service of their masters; and that not only in appearance, but from the heart, as serving God himself. Neither let masters behave morosely and perversely to their servants, harassing them with excessive asperity, or treating them with contempt; but rather acknowledge them as their brethren and companions in the service of the heavenly Master, entitled to be regarded with mutual affection, and to receive kind treatment. In this manner, I say, let every man consider what duties he owes to his neighbours, according to the relations he sustains; and those duties let him discharge. Moreover, our attention should always be directed to the Legislator; to remind us that this law is ordained for our hearts as much as for our hands, in order that men may study both to protect the property and to promote the interests of others.

THE NINTH COMMANDMENT

Thou shalt not bear false witness against thy neighbour.

The end of this precept is, that because God, who is truth   II. viii. 47
itself, execrates a lie, we ought to preserve the truth without the
least disguise. The sum of it therefore is, that we neither violate
the character of any man, either by calumnies or by false accusations, nor distress him in his property by falsehood, nor
injure him by detraction or impertinence. . . . The equity of this
is self-evident. For if a good name be more precious than any
treasures whatever, a man sustains as great an injury when he is
deprived of the integrity of his character, as when he is despoiled
of his wealth. And in plundering his substance, there is sometimes
as much effected by false testimony, as by the hands of violence.
Nevertheless, it is wonderful with what supine security this pre-   II. viii. 48
cept is generally transgressed, so that few persons can be found,
who are not notoriously subject to this malady; we are so fascinated with the malignant pleasure of examining and detecting
the faults of others. Nor should we suppose it to be a sufficient
excuse, that in many cases we cannot be charged with falsehood.
. . . Wherefore, if we possess the true fear and love of God, let us
make it our study, that as far as is practicable and expedient,
and consistent with charity, we devote neither our tongues nor
our ears to opprobrious and malicious raillery, nor inadvertently
attend to unfavourable suspicions; but that, putting fair construc-
tions on every man's words and actions, we regulate our hearts,
our ears, and our tongues, with a view to preserve the reputation of
all around us.

THE TENTH COMMANDMENT

*Thou shalt not covet thy neighbour's house, thou shalt not covet
thy neighbour's wife, nor his man-servant, nor his maid-servant,
nor his ox, nor his ass, nor any thing that is thy neighbour's.*

The end of this precept is, that, since it is the will of God that   II. viii. 49
our whole soul should be under the influence of love, every desire
inconsistent with charity ought to be expelled from our minds.

The sum, then, will be, that no thought should obtrude itself upon us, which would excite in our minds any desire that is noxious, and tends to the detriment of another. To which corresponds the affirmative precept, that all our conceptions, deliberations, resolutions, and undertakings, ought to be consistent with the benefit and advantage of our neighbours. . . . As the Lord . . . has hitherto commanded our wills, efforts, and actions to be subject to the law of love, so now he directs that the conceptions of our minds be subject to the same regulation, lest any of them be corrupt and perverted, and give our hearts an improper impulse. As he has forbidden our minds to be inclined and persuaded to anger, hatred, adultery, rapine, and falsehood, so now he prohibits them from being instigated to these vices. . . .

II. viii. 51   What is the tendency of the whole law, will not now be difficult to judge: it is to a perfection of righteousness, that it may form the life of man after the example of the Divine purity. For God has so delineated his own character in it, that the man who exemplifies in his actions the precepts it contains, will exhibit in his life, as it were, an image of God. . . . The tendency of the doctrine of the law is to connect man with his God, and, as Moses elsewhere expresses it, to make him cleave to the Lord in sanctity of life. (p) Now, the perfection of this sanctity consists in two principal points, already recited — " that we love the Lord our God with all our heart, and with all our soul, and with all our strength, and with all our mind; and our neighbour as ourselves." (q) And the first is, that our souls be completely filled with the love of God. From this the love of our neighbour will naturally follow. . . . He is deceived, therefore, who supposes that the law teaches nothing but certain rudiments and first principles of

II. viii. 54   righteousness. . . . The observance of the commandments consists not in the love of ourselves, but in the love of God and of our neighbour; . . . his is the best and most holy life, who lives as little as possible to himself; and . . . no man leads a worse or more iniquitous life, than he who lives exclusively to himself, and makes his own interest the sole object of his thoughts and pursuits. . . .

(p) Deut. xi. 22.   (q) Luke x. 27.

CHAPTER XIII

The Person of Christ

(1) THE MEDIATOR

SINCE we are fallen from life into death, all that knowledge of II. vi. 1
God as a Creator, of which we have been treating, would be useless,
unless it were succeeded by faith exhibiting God to us as a Father
in Christ. . . . For though God is pleased still to manifest his
paternal kindness to us in various ways, yet we cannot, from a
contemplation of the world, conclude that he is our Father, when
our conscience disturbs us within, and convinces us that our sins
afford a just reason why God should abandon us, and no longer
esteem us as his children. . . . Since the fall of the first man, no
knowledge of God, without the Mediator, has been available to
salvation. . . . And this aggravates the stupidity of those who
set open the gate of heaven to all unbelievers and profane persons,
without the grace of Christ, whom the Scripture universally represents as the only door of entrance into salvation. . . . The hap- II. vi. 2
piness of the Church has always been founded on the person of
Christ. . . . Let this be well fixed in the mind of the reader; II. vi. 4
that the first step to piety is to know that God is our Father, to
protect, govern, and support us till he gathers us into the eternal
inheritance of his kingdom; that hence it is plain . . . that there
can be no saving knowledge of God without Christ, and conse-
quently that from the beginning of the world he has always been

73

manifested to all the elect, that they might look to him, and repose all their confidence in him. . . .

(2) THE NECESSITY OF THE INCARNATION

II. xii. 1   It was of great importance to our interests, that he, who was to be our Mediator, should be both true God and true man. . . . For since our iniquities, like a cloud intervening between us and him, had entirely alienated us from the kingdom of heaven, no one that could not approach to God could be a mediator for the restoration of peace. But who could have approached to him? . . . Our situation was truly deplorable, unless the Divine majesty itself would descend to us; for we could not ascend to it. Thus it was necessary that the Son of God should become Immanuel, that is, God with us; and this in order that there might be a mutual union and coalition between his Divinity and the nature of man; for otherwise the proximity could not be sufficiently near, nor could the affinity be sufficiently strong, to authorize us to hope that God would dwell with us. So great was the discordance between our pollution and the perfect purity of God. . . .

II. xii. 2   It was no mean part which the Mediator had to perform; namely, to restore us to the Divine favour, so as, of children of men, to make us children of God; of heirs of hell, to make us heirs of the kingdom of heaven. Who could accomplish this, unless the Son of God should become also the Son of man, and thus receive to himself what belongs to us, and transfer to us that which is his, and make that which is his by nature ours by grace? . . . Moreover it was highly necessary also for this reason, that he who was to be our Redeemer should be truly both God and man. It was his office to swallow up death; who could do this, but he who was life itself? It was his to overcome sin; who could accomplish this, but righteousness itself? It was his to put to flight the powers of the world and of the air; who could do this, but a power superior both to the world and to the air? Now, who possesses life or righteousness, or the empire and power of heaven, but God alone? Therefore the most merciful God, when he determined on our redemption, became himself our Redeemer in the person of his

II. xii. 3   only begotten Son! . . . Clothed in our flesh, he vanquished sin

and death, in order that the victory and triumph might be ours;
. . . the flesh which he received from us he offered up as a sacrifice, in order to expiate and obliterate our guilt, and appease the
just wrath of the Father.

The persons who consider these things, with the diligent atten-   II. xii. 4
tion which they deserve, will easily disregard vague speculations
which attract minds that are inconstant and fond of novelty. Such
is the notion, that Christ would have become man, even though
the human race had needed no redemption. . . . The end for
which Christ was promised from the beginning, is sufficiently
known; it was to restore a fallen world, and to succour ruined
men. . . . The Scripture no where assigns any other end, for
which the Son of God should choose to become incarnate, and
should also receive this command from the Father, than that he
might be made a sacrifice to appease the Father on our account.
. . . He who feels an eager desire to know something more, not   II. xii. 5
being content with the immutable appointment of God, shows himself also not to be contented with this Christ, who has been given
to us as the price of our redemption. . . . If any adversary object again, that this design of God depended on the fall of man,
which he foresaw, it is abundantly sufficient for me, that every
man is proceeding with impious presumption to imagine to himself a new Christ, whoever he be that permits himself to inquire,
or wishes to know, concerning Christ, any more than God has
predestinated in his secret decree. . . . Paul . . . , after having spoken of the accomplishment of our redemption by Christ,
. . . immediately adds this injunction: "Avoid foolish questions." (*f*) . . .

(3) THE HUMANITY OF CHRIST

The arguments for the Divinity of Christ, which has already   II. xiii. 1
been proved by clear and irrefragable testimonies, it would, I
conceive, be unnecessary to reiterate. It remains, then, for us to
examine, how, after having been invested with our flesh, he had
performed the office of a Mediator. Now, the reality of his humanity was anciently opposed by the Manichæans and by the

---

(*f*) Titus iii. 9.

Marcionites. Of whom the latter imagined to themselves a vision-
ary phantom instead of the body of Christ; and the former dreamed
that he had a celestial body. But both these notions are contrary

II. xiii. 2   to numerous and powerful testimonies of Scripture. . . . Of
whatever cavils either the ancient Manichæans, or their modern
disciples, endeavour to avail themselves, they cannot succeed.
Their nugatory pretence that Christ is called "the Son of man,"
because he was promised to men, is a vain subterfuge; for it is
evident that in the Hebrew idiom, *the Son of man* is a phrase ex-
pressive of a real man. And Christ undoubtedly retained the

II. xiii. 4   phraseology of his own language. . . . The absurdities, with
which these opponents wish to press us, are replete with puerile
cavils. They esteem it mean and dishonourable to Christ, that he
should derive his descent from men; because he could not be
exempt from the universal law, which concludes all the posterity
of Adam, without exception, under sin. (*v*) But the antithesis,
which we find in Paul, easily solves this difficulty: "As by one
man sin entered into the world, and death by sin, even so by the
righteousness of one, the grace of God hath abounded." (*w*) . . .
They betray their ignorance in arguing that, if Christ is perfectly
immaculate, and was begotten of the seed of Mary, by the secret
operation of the Spirit, then it follows that there is no impurity in
the seed of women, but only in that of men. For we do not represent
Christ as perfectly immaculate, merely because he was born of
the seed of a woman unconnected with any man, but because he
was sanctified by the Spirit. . . .

(4) THE TWO NATURES OF CHRIST

II. xiv. 1   When it is said that "the Word was made flesh," (*a*) this is
not to be understood as if the Word was transmuted into flesh, or
blended with flesh. Choosing from the womb of the Virgin a
temple for his residence, he who was the Son of God, became
also the Son of man, not by a confusion of substance, but by a
unity of person. For we assert such a connection and union of the
Divinity with the humanity, that each nature retains its properties

---

(*v*) Gal. iii. 22.   (*w*) Rom. v. 12, 15, 18.   (*a*) John i. 14.

entire, and yet both together constitute one Christ. If any thing among men can be found to resemble so great a mystery, man himself appears to furnish the most apposite similitude; being evidently composed of two substances, of which, however, neither is so confounded with the other, as not to retain its distinct nature. For the soul is not the body, nor is the body the soul. . . . Yet he that is composed of these two parts is no more than one man. . . . There are two different natures united in him to constitute that one person. The Scriptures speak in a similar manner respecting Christ. They attribute to him, sometimes those things which are applicable merely to his humanity; sometimes those things which belong peculiarly to his Divinity; and not unfrequently those things which comprehend both his natures, but are incompatible with either of them alone. And this union of the two natures in Christ they so carefully maintain, that they sometimes attribute to one what belongs to the other — a mode of expression which the ancient writers called a communication of properties. . . .

The clearest of all the passages declarative of the true substance II. xiv 3 of Christ are those which comprehend both the natures together; such as abound in the Gospel of John. For it is not with exclusive reference to the Deity or the humanity, but respecting the complex person composed of both, that we find it there stated; that he has received of the Father power to forgive sins, to raise up whom he will, to bestow righteousness, holiness, and salvation; that he is appointed to be the Judge of the living and the dead, that he may receive the same honour as the Father; (o) finally, that he is "the light of the world," "the good shepherd," "the only door," "the true vine." (p) . . . It is surprising how much ignorant II. xiv. 4 persons, and even some who are not altogether destitute of learning, are perplexed by such forms of expression, as they find attributed to Christ, which are not exactly appropriate either to his Divinity or to his humanity. This is for want of considering that they are applicable to his complex person, consisting of God and man, and to his office of Mediator. . . .

(o) John i. 29; v. 21—23.   (p) John ix. 5; x. 9, 11; xv. 1.

CHAPTER XIV

The Work of Christ

✤

(1) THE THREEFOLD OFFICE

II. xv. 1 **I**T IS a just observation of Augustine, that although heretics profess the name of Christ, yet he is not a foundation to them in common with the pious, but remains exclusively the foundation of the Church; because, on a diligent consideration of what belongs to Christ, Christ will be found among them only in name, not in reality. Thus the Papists in the present age, although the name of the Son of God, the Redeemer of the world, be frequently in their mouths, yet since they are contented with the mere name, and despoil him of his power and dignity, these words of Paul, " not holding the head," (n) are truly applicable to them. Therefore, that faith may find in Christ a solid ground of salvation, and so may rely on him, it is proper for us to establish this principle, that the office which was assigned to him by the Father consists of three parts. For he was given as a Prophet, a King, and a Priest; though we should derive but little benefit from an acquaintance with these names, unaccompanied with a knowledge of their end and use. For they are likewise pronounced among the Papists, but in a frigid and unprofitable manner, while they are ignorant of what is included in each of these titles. . . .

(n) Col. ii. 19.

Now, it is to be observed, that the appellation of " Christ " II. xv. 2
belongs to these three offices. For we know that under the law not
only priests and kings, but prophets also, were anointed with
holy oil. Hence the celebrated title of " Messiah " was given to
the promised Mediator. But though I confess that he was called the
Messiah with particular reference to his kingdom, as I have already shown, yet the prophetical and sacerdotal unctions have
their respective places, and must not be neglected by us. The
former is expressly mentioned by Isaiah in these words: " The
Spirit of the Lord God is upon me; because the Lord hath anointed
me to preach good tidings unto the meek; he hath sent me to bind
up the broken-hearted, to proclaim liberty to the captives, to
proclaim the acceptable year of the Lord." (u) We see that he
was anointed by the Spirit, to be a preacher and witness of the
grace of the Father; and that not in a common manner; for he is
distinguished from other teachers, who held a similar office. . . .
The tendency of the prophetic dignity in Christ is, to assure us that
all the branches of perfect wisdom are included in the system of
doctrine which he has given us.

I come now to his kingdom, of which it would be useless to II. xv. 3
speak, without first apprizing the reader, that it is of a spiritual
nature. . . . Whenever we hear that the kingdom of Christ is
spiritual, excited by this declaration, we ought to penetrate to
the hope of a better life, and as we are now protected by the power
of Christ, let us expect the full benefit of this grace in the world
to come. . . . It ought therefore to be known, that whatever II. xv. 4
felicity is promised us in Christ, consists not in external accommodations, such as a life of joy and tranquillity, abundant wealth,
security from every injury, and numerous delights suited to our
carnal desires, but that it is peculiar to the heavenly state. . . .
Christ enriches his people with every thing necessary to the eternal
salvation of their souls, and arms them with strength to enable
them to stand invincible against all the assaults of their spiritual
foes. Whence we infer that he reigns rather for us than for himself.
. . . Now, as the faithful stand invincible in the strength of their II. xv. 5
King, and are enriched with his spiritual blessings, they are justly
denominated Christians. . . .

(u) Isaiah lxi. 1, 2.

II. xv. 6   Concerning his priesthood, we have briefly to remark, that the end and use of it is, that he may be a Mediator pure from every stain, and by his holiness may render us acceptable to God. But because the righteous curse prevents our access to him, and God in his character of Judge is offended with us, — in order that our Priest may appease the wrath of God, and procure his favour for us, there is a necessity for the intervention of an atonement. Wherefore, that Christ might perform this office, it was necessary for him to appear with a sacrifice. . . . The sacerdotal dignity belongs exclusively to Christ, because, by the sacrifice of his death, he has abolished our guilt, and made satisfaction for our sins. . . . Hence proceeds not only confidence in prayer, but also tranquillity to the consciences of the faithful; while they recline in safety on the paternal indulgence of God, and are certainly persuaded, that he is pleased with whatever is consecrated to him through the Mediator. . . . Christ sustains the character of a Priest, not only to render the Father favourable and propitious to us by an eternal law of reconciliation, but also to associate us with himself in so great an honour. For we, who are polluted in ourselves, being " made priests " (*w*) in him, offer ourselves and all our services to God, and enter boldly into the heavenly sanctuary, so that the sacrifices of prayers and praise, which proceed from us, are " acceptable," and " a sweet-smelling savour " (*x*) in the Divine presence. . . .

(2) THE DEATH, RESURRECTION, AND ASCENSION OF CHRIST

II. xvi. 1   All that we have hitherto advanced concerning Christ is to be referred to this point, that being condemned, dead, and ruined in ourselves, we should seek righteousness, deliverance, life, and salvation in him. . . . But here we ought diligently to examine how he has procured salvation for us; that we may not only know him to be the author of it, but, embracing those things which are sufficient for the establishment of our faith, may reject every

---

(*w*) Rev. i. 6.   (*x*) Eph. v. 2.

thing capable of drawing us aside to the right hand or to the left. . . .

Before we proceed any further, let us examine, by the way, how II. xvi. 2 it could be consistent, that God, who prevents us with his mercy, should be our enemy, till he was reconciled to us by Christ. For how could he have given us a special pledge of his love in his only begotten Son, if he had not previously embraced us in his gratuitous favour? . . . God, who is the perfection of righteous- II. xvi. 3 ness, cannot love iniquity, which he beholds in us all. We all, therefore, have in us that which deserves God's hatred. Wherefore, in respect of our corrupt nature, and the succeeding depravity of our lives, we are all really offensive to God, guilty in his sight, and born to the damnation of hell. But because the Lord will not lose in us that which is his own, he yet discovers something that his goodness may love. For notwithstanding we are sinners through our own fault, yet we are still his creatures; notwithstand- ing we have brought death upon ourselves, yet he had created us for life. Thus, by a pure and gratuitous love towards us, he is ex- cited to receive us into favour. But if there is a perpetual and ir- reconcilable opposition between righteousness and iniquity, he cannot receive us entirely, as long as we remain sinners. There- fore, to remove all occasion of enmity, and to reconcile us com- pletely to himself, he abolishes all our guilt, by the expiation exhibited in the death of Christ, that we, who before were polluted and impure, may appear righteous and holy in his sight. The love of God the Father therefore precedes our reconciliation in Christ; or rather it is because he first loves, that he afterwards rec- onciles us to himself. (e) . . . If we would assure ourselves that God is pacified and propitious to us, we must fix our eyes and hearts on Christ alone, since it is by him only that we really ob- tain the non-imputation of sins, the imputation of which is con- nected with the Divine wrath. . . .

Now, in answer to the inquiry, how Christ, by the abolition of II. xvi. 5 our sins, has destroyed the enmity between God and us, and pro- cured a righteousness to render him favourable and propitious to us, it may be replied in general, that he accomplished it for

---

(e) 1 John iv. 19.

us by the whole course of his obedience. This is proved by the testimony of Paul. "As by one man's disobedience many were made sinners, so by the obedience of one shall many be made righteous." (k) . . . In what is called the Apostles' Creed, there is very properly an immediate transition from the birth of Christ to his death and resurrection, in which the sum of perfect salvation consists. Yet there is no exclusion of the rest of the obedience which he performed in his life; as Paul comprehends the whole of it, from the beginning to the end, when he says, that " he made himself of no reputation, and took upon him the form of a servant, and became obedient unto death, even the death of the cross." (t) And indeed his voluntary submission is the principal circumstance even in his death; because the sacrifice, unless freely offered, would have been unavailable to the acquisition of righteousness. . . . This is our absolution, that the guilt, which made us obnoxious to punishment, is transferred to the person of the Son of God. For we ought particularly to remember this satisfaction, that we may not spend our whole lives in terror and anxiety, as though we were pursued by the righteous vengeance of God, which the Son of God has transferred to himself. . . .

II. xvi. 7   It follows in the Creed, "that he died and was buried;" in which may be further seen, how in every respect he substituted himself in our room to pay the price of our redemption. Death held us in bondage under his yoke; Christ, to deliver us from it, surrendered himself to his power in our stead. This is the meaning of the apostle, when he says, that " he tasted death for every man." (r) For by his death he prevented us from dying, or, which comes to the same thing, by his death recovered life for us. But in this respect he differed from us — he surrendered himself to death to be, as it were, overcome by it, not that he might be absorbed in its abysses, but rather that he might destroy that, by which we should have been at length devoured; he surrendered himself to death to be subdued, not that he might be overwhelmed by its power, but rather that he might overthrow that which threatened us, which indeed had already overcome us, and was triumphing over us. . . .

(k) Rom. v. 19.   (t) Phil. ii. 7, 8.   (r) Heb. ii. 9.

It is not right to omit his "descent into hell," which is of no II. xvi. 8
small importance towards the accomplishment of redemption.
For though it appears from the writings of the ancients, that this
article of the Creed was not always in common use in the churches,
yet in discussing a system of doctrine, it is necessary to introduce
it, as containing a mystery highly useful, and by no means to be
despised. . . . If Christ had merely died a corporeal death, no II. xvi. 10
end would have been accomplished by it; it was requisite, also,
that he should feel the severity of the Divine vengeance, in order
to appease the wrath of God, and satisfy his justice. Hence it was
necessary for him to contend with the powers of hell and the
horror of eternal death. . . . He suffered in his soul the dreadful
torments of a person condemned and irretrievably lost. . . . We II. xvi. 11
see Christ was so deeply dejected, that in the urgency of distress,
he was constrained to exclaim, "My God, my God, why hast thou
forsaken me?" (f) . . .

Next follows his resurrection from the dead, without which II. xvi. 13
all that we have said would be incomplete. . . . Wherefore, although our salvation is perfectly accomplished by his death,
because by that we are reconciled to God, a satisfaction is given to
his righteous judgment, the curse is removed, and the punishment
sustained, yet we are said to have been "begotten again to a lively
hope," not by his death, but "by his resurrection from the dead."
(p) For as at his resurrection he appeared the conqueror of death,
so it is on his resurrection that our faith principally rests. . . .
Wherefore we ascribe our salvation partly to the death of Christ,
and partly to his resurrection; we believe that sin was abolished,
and death destroyed, by the former; that righteousness was
restored, and life established, by the latter; yet so that the former
discovers its power and efficacy in us by means of the latter. . . .

His *resurrection* is properly followed in the Creed by his *ascen-* II. xvi. 14
sion to heaven. For though Christ began to make a more illustri-
ous display of his glory and power at his resurrection, having
now laid aside the abject and ignoble condition of this mortal life,
and the ignominy of the cross, yet his ascension into heaven was
the real commencement of his reign. . . . Wherefore it is II. xvi. 15

(f) Matt. xxvii. 46.   (p) 1 Peter i. 3.

immediately added, *that he is seated at the right hand of the Father;* which is a similitude borrowed from princes, who have their assistants, to whom they depute the exercise of the government. So Christ, in whom the Father determines to be exalted, and by whose medium he chooses to reign, is said to have been received to his right hand; as though it were said, that he had been inaugurated in the government of heaven and earth, and had solemnly entered on the actual administration of the power committed to him; and not only that he has entered on it, but that he continues in it, till he descends to judgment. . . . Christ gives his servants unequivocal tokens of the presence of his power; but because on earth his kingdom is in some measure concealed under the meanness of the flesh, faith is, for a very good reason, called to meditate on that visible presence which he will manifest at the last day. . . . From thence, therefore, we are commanded to expect him as our Redeemer at the last day, when he will separate the sheep from the goats, the elect from the reprobate; and there will not be an individual of either the living or the dead that can escape his judgment. . . . It is a source of peculiar consolation to hear that he will preside at the judgment, who has already destined us to participate with himself the honour of sitting in judgment with him, so far will he be from ascending the tribunal to condemn us. For how could a most merciful prince destroy his own people? how could a head scatter his own members? how could an advocate condemn his own clients? . . .

Since we see that the whole of our salvation, and all the branches of it, are comprehended in Christ, we must be cautious not to alienate from him the least possible portion of it. If we seek salvation, we are taught by the name of JESUS, that it is in him; if we seek any other gifts of the Spirit, they will be found in his unction; strength, in his dominion; purity, in his conception; indulgence discovers itself in his nativity, by which he was made to resemble us in all things, that he might learn to condole with us; if we seek redemption, it will be found in his passion; absolution, in his condemnation; remission of the curse, in his cross; satisfaction, in his sacrifice; purification, in his blood; reconciliation, in his descent into hell; mortification of the flesh, in his sepulchre; newness of life and immortality, in his resurrection; the inherit-

II. xvi. 17

II. xvi. 18

II. xvi. 19

ance of the celestial kingdom, in his entrance into heaven; protection, security, abundance, and enjoyment of all blessings, in his kingdom; a fearless expectation of the judgment, in the judicial authority committed to him. Finally blessings of every kind are deposited in him; let us draw from his treasury, and from no other source, till our desires are satisfied. . . .

(3) SALVATION THROUGH CHRIST

There are some . . . , more subtle than orthodox, who, though they confess that Christ obtained salvation for us, yet cannot bear the word *merit*, by which they suppose the grace of God is obscured. So they maintain that Christ is only the instrument or minister, not, as he is called by Peter, the Author, or Leader, and "Prince of life." (*q*) . . . When we speak of the merit of Christ . . . we do not consider him as the origin of it, but we ascend to the ordination of God, which is the first cause; because it was of his mere good pleasure, that God appointed him Mediator to procure salvation for us. And thus it betrays ignorance to oppose the merit of Christ to the mercy of God. . . . Since the merit of Christ depends solely on the grace of God, which appointed this method of salvation for us, therefore his merit and that grace are with equal propriety opposed to all the righteousnesses of men. This distinction is gathered from numerous passages of Scripture. "God so loved the world, that he gave his only begotten Son, that whosoever believeth in him should not perish." (*r*) We see that the love of God holds the first place, as the supreme and original cause, and that faith in Christ follows as the second and proximate cause. . . . If Christ has satisfied for our sins; if he has sustained the punishment due to us; if he has appeased God by his obedience; in a word, if he has suffered, the just for the unjust, — then salvation has been obtained for us by his righteousness. . . .

II. xvii. 1

II. xvii. 2

II. xvii. 3

(*q*) Acts iii. 15.   (*r*) John iii. 16.

Book III

The Holy Spirit

CHAPTER XV

The Work of the Holy Spirit

(1) SALVATION

W E ARE now to examine how we obtain the enjoyment of those III. i. 1
blessings which the Father has conferred on his only begotten
Son, not for his own private use, but to enrich the poor and needy.
And first it must be remarked, that as long as there is a separation
between Christ and us, all that he suffered and performed for the
salvation of mankind is useless and unavailing to us. To communicate to us what he received from his Father, he must, therefore,
become ours, and dwell within us. . . . But though it be true that
we obtain this by faith, yet, since we see that the communication
of Christ, offered in the gospel, is not promiscuously embraced
by all, reason itself teaches us to proceed further, and to inquire
into the secret energy of the Spirit, by which we are introduced
to the enjoyment of Christ and all his benefits. . . . The Holy
Spirit is the bond by which Christ efficaciously unites us to himself. . . . We must remember that Christ was endued with the III. i. 2
Holy Spirit in a peculiar manner; in order to separate us from the
world, and introduce us into the hope of an eternal inheritance.
. . . The principal topic, therefore, dwelt on by the prophets in
celebrating the kingdom of Christ, is, that there would then be
a more exuberant effusion of the Spirit. . . . As God the Father
gives us his Holy Spirit for the sake of his Son, and yet has

deposited " all fulness " with his Son, that he might be the minister and dispenser of his own goodness, — the Holy Spirit is sometimes called the Spirit of the Father, and sometimes the Spirit
of the Son. . . .

III. i. 3   It will be proper to notice the titles by which the Scripture distinguishes the Spirit. . . . First, he is called the " Spirit of adoption; " (r) . . . he is said to be " the earnest " and " seal " of our
inheritance; (s) . . . he is also said to be " life," because of
righteousness; (t) . . . he is frequently called " water; " as in
Isaiah: " Ho, every one that thirsteth, come ye to the waters; "
(u) . . . he is . . . called " fire." (a) Lastly, he is described
to us as a " fountain," whence we receive all the emanation of
heavenly riches; and as " the hand of God," by which he exerts
his power; because by the breath of his power he inspires us with
Divine life, so that we are not now actuated from ourselves, but
directed by his agency and influence; so that if there be any good
in us, it is the fruit of his grace, whereas our characters without
him are darkness of mind and perverseness of heart. It has, indeed,
already been clearly stated, that till our minds are fixed on the
Spirit, Christ remains of no value to us; because we look at him as
an object of cold speculation without us, and therefore at a great
distance from us. But we know that he benefits none but those who
have him for their " head " and " elder brother," and who have
" put him on." (b) This union alone renders his advent in the
character of a Saviour available to us. We learn the same truth
from that sacred marriage, by which we are made flesh of his flesh
and bone of his bone, and therefore one with him. (c) It is only
by his Spirit that he unites himself with us; and by the grace and
power of the same Spirit we are made his members; that he may
III. i. 4   keep us under himself, and we may mutually enjoy him. But
faith, being his principal work, is the object principally referred
to in the most frequent expressions of his power and operation.
. . . In vain would the light present itself to the blind, unless this
Spirit of understanding would open their mental eyes; so that he
may be justly called the key with which the treasures of the king-

---

(r) Rom. viii. 15.   (s) 2 Cor. i. 22.   Eph. i. 13, 14.   (t) Rom. viii. 10.
     (u) Isaiah lv. 1.   (a) Luke iii. 16.
     (b) Eph. iv. 15.   Rom. viii. 29.   Gal. iii. 27.   (c) Eph. v. 30.

dom of heaven are unlocked to us; and his illumination constitutes our mental eyes to behold them. . . .

(2) FAITH

A great part of the world, when they hear the word *faith,* con- III. ii. 1
ceive it to be nothing more than a common assent to the evangelical history. . . . Faith consists not in ignorance, but in III. ii. 2
knowledge; and that not only of God, but also of the Divine will.
For we do not obtain salvation by our promptitude to embrace as
truth whatever the Church may have prescribed, or by our trans-
ferring to her the province of inquiry and of knowledge. . . . We III. ii. 4
grant, that during our pilgrimage in the world, our faith is implicit, not only because many things are yet hidden from our view,
but because our knowledge of every thing is very imperfect, in
consequence of the clouds of error by which we are surrounded.
. . . We may also style that an implicit faith, which in strict pro- III. ii. 5
priety is nothing but a preparation for faith. . . . Faith has a III. ii. 6
perpetual relation to the word, and can no more be separated from
it, than the rays from the sun, whence they proceed. . . . Take
away the word, then, and there will be no faith left. . . . The word
itself, however it may be conveyed to us, is like a mirror, in which
faith may behold God. . . . The apprehension of faith is not confined to our knowing that there is a God, but chiefly consists in our
understanding what is his disposition towards us. For it is not of
so much importance to us to know what he is in himself, as what
he is willing to be to us. We find, therefore, that faith is a knowledge of the will of God respecting us, received from his word. . . .

Our mind must be illuminated, and our heart established by III. ii. 7
some exterior power, that the word of God may obtain full credit
with us. Now, we shall have a complete definition of faith, if we
say, that it is a steady and certain knowledge of the Divine benevolence towards us, which, being founded on the truth of the gratuitous promise in Christ, is both revealed to our minds, and confirmed to our hearts, by the Holy Spirit. . . . Now, let us . . . III. ii. 14
examine all the parts of that definition. . . . When we call it
knowledge, we intend not such a comprehension as men commonly
have of those things which fall under the notice of their senses.

. . . Nor does the mind which attains it comprehend what it perceives, but being persuaded of that which it cannot comprehend, it understands more by the certainty of this persuasion, than it would comprehend of any human object by the exercise of its natural capacity. . . . The knowledge of faith consists more in

III. ii. 15   certainty than in comprehension. To express the solid constancy of the persuasion, we further say, that it is a certain and steady knowledge. For, as faith is not content with a dubious and versatile opinion, so neither with an obscure and perplexed conception; but requires a full and fixed certainty, such as is commonly ob-

III. ii. 16   tained respecting things that have been tried and proved. . . . No man is truly a believer, unless he be firmly persuaded, that God is a propitious and benevolent Father to him, and promise himself every thing from his goodness; unless he depend on the promises of the Divine benevolence to him, and feel an undoubted expecta-

III. ii. 17   tion of salvation. . . . When we inculcate, that faith ought to be certain and secure, we conceive not of a certainty attended with no doubt, or of a security interrupted by no anxiety; but we rather affirm, that believers have a perpetual conflict with their own diffidence, and are far from placing their consciences in a placid calm, never disturbed by any storms. Yet, on the other hand, we deny, however they may be afflicted, that they ever fall and depart from that certain confidence which they have conceived in the Divine mercy. . . . He who, contending with his own infirmity, strives in his anxieties to exercise faith, is already in a great measure vic-

III. ii. 21   torious. . . . Unbelief is not inwardly predominant. in the hearts of the pious, but it assails them from without; nor do its weapons mortally wound them; they only molest them, or at least inflict such wounds as are curable. . . .

III. ii. 28   In the Divine benevolence, which is affirmed to be the object of faith, we apprehend the possession of salvation and everlasting life to be obtained. For, if no good can be wanting when God is propitious, we have a sufficient certainty of salvation, when he himself assures us of his love. . . . Faith, having apprehended the love of God, has promises for the present life and the life to come, and a solid assurance of all blessings. . . . God will never leave us. . . . Whatever miseries and calamities may on earth await those who are the objects of the love of God, they cannot prevent the Divine benevolence from being a source of complete felicity. . . .

We make the foundation of faith to be the gratuitous promise; for on that faith properly rests. . . . If we wish our faith not to tremble and waver, we must support it with the promise of salvation, which is voluntarily and liberally offered us by the Lord, rather in consideration of our misery, than in respect of our worthiness. . . .   III. ii. 29

Such is our propensity to error, that our mind can never adhere to Divine truth; such is our dulness, that we can never discern the light of it. Therefore nothing is effected by the word, without the illumination of the Holy Spirit. Whence it appears, that faith is far superior to human intelligence. Nor is it enough for the mind to be illuminated by the Spirit of God, unless the heart also be strengthened and supported by his power. On this point, the school-men are altogether erroneous, who, in the discussion of faith, regard it as a simple assent of the understanding, entirely neglecting the confidence and assurance of the heart. Faith, therefore, is a singular gift of God in two respects; both as the mind is enlightened to understand the truth of God, and as the heart is established in it. For the Holy Spirit not only originates faith, but increases it by degrees, till he conducts us by it all the way to the heavenly kingdom. . . . For illuminated by him, the soul receives, as it were, new eyes for the contemplation of heavenly mysteries, by the splendour of which it was before dazzled. . . . The word of God is like the sun shining on all to whom it is preached; but without any benefit to the blind. But in this respect we are all blind by nature; therefore it cannot penetrate into our minds, unless the internal teacher, the Spirit, make way for it by his illumination. . . . Augustine . . . says, " It was in order to teach us that the act of believing is owing to the Divine gift, not to human merit, that our Saviour declared, ' No man can come to me, except the Father which has sent me draw him; (o) and except it were given unto him of my Father.' (p) It is wonderful, that two persons hear; one despises, the other ascends. Let him who despises, impute it to himself; let him who ascends, not arrogate it to himself." . . .   III. ii. 33   III. ii. 34   III. ii. 35

(o) John vi. 44.   (p) John vi. 65.

III. ii. 36   It next remains, that what the mind has imbibed, be transfused into the heart. For the word of God is not received by faith, if it floats on the surface of the brain; but when it has taken deep root in the heart, so as to become an impregnable fortress to sustain and repel all the assaults of temptation. . . . The Spirit acts as a seal, to seal on our hearts those very promises, the certainty of which he has previously impressed on our minds, and serves as an earnest to confirm and establish them. . . .

III. ii. 42   Now, wherever this living faith shall be found, it must necessarily be attended with the hope of eternal salvation as its inseparable concomitant, or rather must originate and produce it; since the want of this hope would prove us to be utterly destitute of faith, however eloquently and beautifully we might discourse concerning it. . . . Hope is no other than an expectation of those things which faith has believed to be truly promised by God. Thus faith believes the veracity of God, hope expects the manifestation of it in due time; faith believes him to be our Father, hope expects him always to act towards us in this character; faith believes that eternal life is given to us, hope expects it one day to be revealed; faith is the foundation on which hope rests, hope nourishes and sustains faith. . . .

(3) REPENTANCE

III. iii. 1   Though we have already shown, in some respect, how faith possesses Christ, and how by means of faith we enjoy his benefits, yet the subject would still be involved in obscurity, unless we were to add a description of the effects which we experience. . . . Now, it ought not to be doubted that repentance not only immediately follows faith, but is produced by it. . . . No one can embrace the grace of the gospel, but he must depart from the errors of his former life, enter into the right way, and devote all his attention to the exercise of repentance. Those who imagine that repentance rather precedes faith, than is produced by it, as fruit by a tree, have never been acquainted with its power, and are induced to adopt that sentiment by a very insufficient argument.

III. iii. 2   They argue that Jesus Christ and John the Baptist, in their preaching, first exhort the people to repentance; and afterwards add, that

" the kingdom of heaven is at hand; " (e) . . . but they super-
stitiously attend to the connection of the syllables, and disregard
the sense and coherence of the words. . . . The meaning of their
language . . . is just as though they had said, Since the kingdom
of heaven is at hand, therefore repent. . . . A man cannot truly
devote himself to repentance, unless he knows himself to be of
God. Now, no man is truly persuaded that he is of God, except he
has previously received his grace. . . .

But concerning repentance, some learned men, in times very   III. iii. 3
remote from the present, desiring to express themselves with
simplicity and sincerity according to the rule of the Scripture,
have said that it consists of two parts — mortification and vivification. Mortification they explain to be the sorrow of the mind,
and the terror experienced from a knowledge of sin and a sense of
the Divine judgments. . . . Vivification they explain to be the
consolation which is produced by faith. . . . Others, perceiving   III. iii. 4
[repentance] . . . to have various acceptations in Scripture, have
laid down two kinds of repentance; and, to distinguish them by
some character, have called one Legal; in which the sinner,
wounded by the envenomed dart of sin, and harassed by the fear
of Divine wrath, is involved in deep distress, without the power
of extricating himself: the other they style Evangelical; in which
the sinner is grievously afflicted in himself, but rises above his
distress, and embraces Christ as the medicine for his wound, the
consolation of his terrors, and his refuge from all misery. . . .
Though all these observations are true, yet the term *repentance*,   III. iii. 5
as far as I can ascertain from the Scriptures, must have a different
acceptation. For to include faith in repentance, is repugnant to
what Paul says in the Acts — that he testified " both to the Jews,
and also to the Greeks, repentance toward God, and faith toward
our Lord Jesus Christ; " (r) where he mentions faith and repentance, as two things totally distinct. What then? Can true repentance exist without faith? Not at all. But though they cannot
be separated yet they ought to be distinguished. As faith exists
not without hope, and yet there is a difference between them, so
repentance and faith, although they are perpetually and indissolubly united, require to be connected rather than confounded. . . .

(e) Matt. iii. 2; iv. 17.   (r) Acts xx. 21.

The Hebrew word for repentance denotes conversion or return. The Greek word signifies change of mind and intention. Repentance itself corresponds very well with both etymologies, for it comprehends these two things — that, forsaking ourselves, we should turn to God, and laying aside our old mind, should assume a new one. Wherefore I conceive it may be justly defined to be *" a true conversion of our life to God, proceeding from a sincere and serious fear of God, and consisting in the mortification of our flesh and of the old man, and in the vivification of the Spirit."* . . .

III. iii. 6   It will be useful to amplify and explain the definition we have given; in which there are three points to be particularly considered. In the first place, when we call repentance " a conversion of the life to God," we require a transformation, not only in the external actions, but in the soul itself; which, after having put off its old nature, should produce the fruits of actions corresponding

III. iii. 7   to its renovation. . . . In the second place, we represented repentance as proceeding from a serious fear of God. For before the mind of a sinner can be inclined to repentance, it must be excited

III. iii. 8   by a knowledge of the Divine judgment. . . . It remains for us, in the third place, to explain our position, that repentance consists of two parts — the mortification of the flesh and the vivifica-

III. iii. 9   tion of the spirit. . . . Both these branches of repentance are effects of our participation of Christ. For if we truly partake of his death, our old man is crucified by its power, and the body of sin expires, so that the corruption of our former nature loses all its vigour. (e) If we are partakers of his resurrection, we are raised by it to a newness of life, which corresponds with the righteousness of God. In one word I apprehend repentance to be regeneration, the end of which is the restoration of the Divine image within us; which was defaced, and almost obliterated, by the transgression of Adam. . . . This restoration is not accomplished in a single moment, or day, or year; but by continual, and sometimes even tardy advances, the Lord destroys the carnal corruptions of his chosen, purifies them from all pollution, and consecrates them as temples to himself; renewing all their senses to real purity, that they may employ their whole life in the exercise of repentance,

---

(e) Rom. vi. 5, 6

and know that this warfare will be terminated only by death. . . . There still remains in a regenerate man a fountain of evil, con- III. iii. 10 tinually producing irregular desires, which allure and stimulate him to the commission of sin. . . .

When the apostle, in a description of repentance, enumerates III. iii. 15 seven things, which are either causes producing it, or effects proceeding from it, or members and parts of it, he does it for a very good reason. These things are, carefulness, excuse, indignation, fear, vehement desire, zeal, revenge. (q) . . . He says . . . that godly sorrow produces *solicitude*. For a person who is affected with a serious sense of displeasure because he has sinned against his God, is at the same time stimulated to diligence and attention, that he may completely extricate himself from the snares of the devil. . . . The next thing is *self-excuse*, which in this place signifies not a defence by which a sinner tries to escape the judgment of God, either by denying his transgressions or extenuating his guilt, but a kind of excuse, consisting rather in deprecation of punishment than in confidence of his cause. . . . This is followed by *indignation*, in which the sinner laments within himself, expostulates with himself, and is angry with himself, while he recollects his perverseness and ingratitude to God. The word *fear* denotes that trepidation with which our minds are penetrated, whenever we reflect upon our demerits, and on the terrible severity of the Divine wrath against sinners. . . . He appears to me to have used the word *desire* to denote diligence in duty and alacrity of obedience. . . . Similar to this is the meaning of *zeal*, which he immediately subjoins; for it signifies the ardour with which we are inflamed. . . . The last thing is *revenge*, or punishment. . . . A soul, impressed with a dread of the Divine judgment, must inflict some punishment on itself. Truly pious persons experience what punishments are contained in shame, confusion, lamentation, displeasure with themselves, and the other affections. . . .

Now, it may also be understood what are the fruits of repent- III. iii. 16 ance. They are, the duties of piety towards God, and of charity towards men, with sanctity and purity in our whole life. . . .

(q) 2 Cor. vii. 11.

CHAPTER XVI

The Christian Life

(1) RELIGION AND LIFE

III. vi. 1   W E HAVE said that the end of regeneration is, that the life of believers may exhibit a symmetry and agreement between the righteousness of God and their obedience; and that thus they may confirm the adoption by which they are accepted as his children. But though the law of God contains in it that newness of life by which his image is restored in us, yet since our tardiness needs much stimulation and assistance, it will be useful to collect from various places of Scripture a rule for the reformation of the life, that they who cordially repent may not be bewildered in their pursuits. . . . It will be sufficient for me if I point out a method by which a pious man may be conducted to the right end in the regulation of his life, and briefly assign a universal rule, by which he may properly estimate his duties. . . . As the philosophers have certain principles of rectitude and honour, whence they deduce particular duties and the whole circle of virtues, so the Scripture is not without its order in this respect, but maintains an economy superlatively beautiful, and far more certain, than all

III. vi. 2   the systems of the philosophers. . . . This Scripture plan, of which we are now treating, consists chiefly in these two things — the first, that a love of righteousness, to which we have otherwise no natural propensity, be instilled and introduced into our hearts;

98

the second that a rule be prescribed to us, to prevent our taking any devious steps in the race of righteousness. Now, in the recommendation of righteousness, it uses a great number of very excellent arguments. . . . With what better foundation can it begin, than when it admonishes us that we ought to be holy, because *our God is holy?* (*w*) . . . And as a further incitement to us, it III. vi. 3 shows, that as God the Father has reconciled us to himself in Christ, so he has exhibited to us in him a pattern, to which it is his will that we should be conformed. (*z*)

Now, let those who are of opinion that the philosophers have the only just and orderly systems of moral philosophy, show me, in any of their works, a more excellent economy than that which I have stated. When they intend to exhort us to the sublimest virtue, they advance no argument but that we ought to live agreeably to nature; but the Scripture deduces its exhortation from the true source, when it not only enjoins us to refer our life to God the author of it, to whom it belongs, but, after having taught us, that we are degenerated from the original state in which we were created, adds, that Christ, by whom we have been reconciled to God, is proposed to us as an example, whose character we should exhibit in our lives. . . . This is a proper place to address those III. vi. 4 who have nothing but the name and the symbol of Christ, and yet would be denominated Christians. But with what face do they glory in his sacred name? For none have any intercourse with Christ but those who have received the true knowledge of him from the word of the gospel. . . . Let them, therefore, either cease to insult God by boasting themselves to be what they are not, or show themselves disciples not unworthy of Christ, their Master. . . . Yet I would not insist upon it as absolutely necessary, that III. vi. 5 the manners of a Christian should breathe nothing but the perfect gospel; which, nevertheless, ought both to be wished and to be aimed at. But I do not so rigorously require evangelical perfection as not to acknowledge as a Christian, one who has not yet attained to it; for then all would be excluded from the Church; since no man can be found who is not still at a great distance from it; and many have hitherto made but a very small progress,

---

(*w*) Lev. xix. 2.   1 Peter i. 16.   (*z*) Rom. vi. 4, &c.; viii. 29.

whom it would, nevertheless, be unjust to reject. What then? let us set before our eyes that mark, to which alone our pursuit must be directed. Let that be prescribed as the goal towards which we must earnestly tend. For it is not lawful for you to make such a compromise with God, as to undertake a part of the duties prescribed to you in his word, and to omit part of them, at your own pleasure. For, in the first place, he every where recommends integrity as a principal branch of his worship; by which he intends a sincere simplicity of heart, free from all guile and falsehood; the opposite of which is a double heart; as though it had been said, that the beginning of a life of uprightness is spiritual, when the internal affection of the mind is unfeignedly devoted to God in the cultivation of holiness and righteousness. But since no man in this terrestrial and corporeal prison has strength sufficient to press forward in his course with a due degree of alacrity, and the majority are oppressed with such great debility, that they stagger and halt, and even creep on the ground, and so make very inconsiderable advances, — let us every one proceed according to our small ability, and prosecute the journey we have begun. No man will be so unhappy, but that he may every day make some progress, however small. Therefore, let us not cease to strive, that we may be incessantly advancing in the way of the Lord; nor let us despair on account of the smallness of our success; for however our success may not correspond to our wishes, yet our labour is not lost, when this day surpasses the preceding one; provided that, with sincere simplicity, we keep our end in view, and press forward to the goal, not practising self-adulation, nor indulging our own evil propensities, but perpetually exerting our endeavours after increasing degrees of amelioration, till we shall have arrived at a perfection of goodness, which, indeed, we seek and pursue as long as we live, and shall then attain, when, divested of all corporeal infirmity, we shall be admitted by God into complete communion with him.

(2) CHRISTIAN SELF–DENIAL

III. vii. 1   Although the Divine law contains a most excellent and well-arranged plan for the regulation of life, yet it has pleased the heavenly Teacher to conform men by a more accurate doctrine to the rule which he had prescribed in the law. And the principle of that doctrine is this — that it is the duty of believers to " present their bodies a living sacrifice, holy, acceptable unto God." (b) . . . We are not our own; therefore neither our reason nor our will should predominate in our deliberations and actions. We are not our own; therefore let us not propose it as our end, to seek what may be expedient for us according to the flesh. We are not our own; therefore let us, as far as possible, forget ourselves and all things that are ours. On the contrary, we are God's; to him, therefore, let us live and die. We are God's; therefore let his wisdom and will preside in all our actions. We are God's; towards him, therefore, as our only legitimate end, let every part of our lives be directed. . . .

Let this, then, be the first step, to depart from ourselves, that we may apply all the vigour of our faculties to the service of the Lord. By service I mean, not that only which consists in verbal obedience, but that by which the human mind, divested of its natural carnality, resigns itself wholly to the direction of the Divine Spirit. . . . Hence also that other consequence, III. vii. 2 that we should seek not our own things, but those which are agreeable to the will of the Lord, and conducive to the promotion of his glory. . . . The result of attention to these directions will be, that III. vii. 4 with whomsoever we are concerned, we shall conduct ourselves not only with moderation and good humour, but with civility and friendship. For we shall never arrive at true meekness by any other way, than by having our hearts imbued with self-abasement and a respect for others. . . .

There cannot be imagined a more certain rule, or a more power- III. vii. 5 ful exhortation to the observance of it, than when we are taught, that all the blessings we enjoy are Divine deposits, committed to our trust on this condition, that they should be dispensed for the benefit of our neighbours. . . . Whatever God has conferred on us, which enables us to assist our neighbour, we are the stewards of it, and must one day render an account of our stewardship; and that the only right dispensation of what has been committed to us,

---

(b) Rom. xii. 1.

III. vii. 6 is that which is regulated by the law of love. . . . Moreover, that we may not be weary of doing good, which otherwise would of necessity soon be the case, we must add also the other character mentioned by the apostle, that " charity suffereth long, and is not easily provoked." . . . We should remember, that we must not reflect on the wickedness of men, but contemplate the Divine image in them; which, concealing and obliterating their faults, by its beauty and dignity allures us to embrace them in the arms of our

III. vii. 7 love. . . . The duties of charity . . . are fulfilled, not by him who merely performs all the external offices of charity, even without the omission of one, but by him who does this from a sincere principle of love. For it may happen, that a man may fully discharge his duty to all men, with respect to external actions, and, at the same time, be very far from discharging it in the right way.

III. vii. 9 . . . If we believe that all the cause of desirable prosperity consists in the Divine benediction alone, without which miseries and calamities of every kind await us, it follows also, that we should not passionately strive for wealth and honours, either relying on our own diligence or acuteness of understanding, or depending on the favour of men, or confiding in a vain imagination of chance; but that we should always regard the Lord, to be conducted by his direction to whatsoever lot he has provided for us. The consequence of this will be, in the first place, that we shall not rush forward to seize in wealth or honours by unlawful actions, by deceitful and criminal arts, by rapacity and injury of our neighbours; but shall confine ourselves to the pursuit of those interests, which will not seduce us from the path of innocence. . . . We shall find a restraint laid upon us, to keep us from being inflamed with an inordinate desire of growing rich, and from ambitiously aspiring after honours. . . . If our success be not equal to our wishes and hopes, yet we shall be restrained from impatience. . . .

III. vii. 10 The same state of mind ought to be extended to all the events to which the present life is exposed. Therefore no man has rightly renounced himself, but he who has wholly resigned himself to the Lord, so as to leave all the parts of his life to be governed by his will. He whose mind is thus composed, whatever may befall him, will neither think himself miserable, nor invidiously complain against God on account of his lot. . . .

All whom the Lord has chosen and honoured with admission   III. viii. 1
into the society of his saints, ought to prepare themselves for a
life, hard, laborious, unquiet, and replete with numerous and various calamities. It is the will of their heavenly Father to exercise
them in this manner, that he may have a certain proof of those that
belong to him. . . . Our Lord was under no necessity of bearing   III. viii. 2
the cross, except to testify and prove his obedience to his Father;
but there are many reasons which render it necessary for us to live
under a continual cross. . . . We easily form an extravagant estimate of our strength, presuming that whatever may happen, it will
remain undaunted and invincible amidst all difficulties. This in-
flates us with a foolish, vain, carnal confidence. . . . This arrogance [God] . . . cannot better repress, than by proving to us
from experience, not only our great imbecility, but also our extreme frailty. Therefore he afflicts us with ignominy, or poverty, or
loss of relatives, or disease, or other calamities; to the bearing of
which being in ourselves unequal, we ere long sink under them.
Thus being humbled, we learn to invoke his strength, which alone
causes us to stand erect under a load of afflictions. . . . The Lord   III. viii. 4
has also another end in afflicting his children; to try their patience,
and teach them obedience. Not, indeed, that they can perform any
other obedience to him than that which he has given them; but he
is pleased in this manner, by clear evidences, to exhibit and testify
the graces which he has conferred on his saints, that they may not
be concealed in inactivity within them. . . . But it is a source of   III. viii. 7
peculiar consolation when we suffer persecution " for righteousness' sake." (g) For we ought then to reflect how greatly we are
honoured by God, when he thus distinguishes us with the peculiar
characteristic of his service. . . . For if, being innocent and conscious of our own integrity, we are stripped of our property by the
villany of the wicked, we are reduced to poverty indeed among
men, but we thereby obtain an increase of true riches with God in
heaven; if we are banished from our country, we are more intimately received into the family of God; if we meet with vexation
and contempt, we are so much the more firmly rooted in Christ; if
we are stigmatized with reproach and ignominy, we are so much the

---

(g) Matt. v. 10.

more exalted in the kingdom of God; if we are massacred, it opens an entrance for us into a life of blessedness. We ought to be ashamed of setting a lower estimation on things on which the Lord has attached such a great value, than on the shadowy and evanescent pleasures of the present life. . . .

(3) THE GOOD LIFE AND THE LIFE TO COME

III. ix. 1   With whatever kind of tribulation we may be afflicted, we should always keep this end in view — to habituate ourselves to a contempt of the present life, that we may thereby be excited to meditation on that which is to come. . . . There is not one of us who is not desirous of appearing, through the whole course of his life, to aspire and strive after celestial immortality. . . . But . . . the . . . soul, fascinated by carnal allurements, seeks its felicity on earth. To oppose this evil, the Lord, by continual lessons of miseries, teaches his children the vanity of the present life. That they may not promise themselves profound and secure peace in it, therefore he permits them to be frequently disquieted and infested with wars or tumults, with robberies or other injuries. That they may not aspire with too much avidity after transient and uncertain riches, or depend on those which they possess, — sometimes by exile, sometimes by the sterility of the land, sometimes by a conflagration, sometimes by other means, he reduces them to indigence, or at least confines them within the limits of mediocrity. That they may not be too complacently delighted with conjugal blessings, he either causes them to be distressed with the wickedness of their wives, or humbles them with a wicked offspring, or afflicts them with want or loss of children. But if in all these things he is more indulgent to them, yet that they may not be inflated with vain glory, or improper confidence, he shows them by diseases and dangers the unstable and transitory nature of all mortal blessings. . . . Therefore . . . we learn that this life, considered in itself, is unquiet, turbulent, miserable in numberless instances, and in no respect altogether happy; and that all its reputed blessings are uncertain, transient, vain, and adulterated with a mixture of many evils; and in consequence of this at once conclude, that nothing

can be sought or expected on earth but conflict, and that when we
think of a crown we must raise our eyes towards heaven. . . .

But believers should accustom themselves to such a contempt of   III. ix. 3
the present life, as may not generate either hatred of life, or ingratitude towards God. For this life, though it is replete with innumerable miseries, is yet deservedly reckoned among the Divine
blessings which must not be despised. . . . It is a . . . reason
for gratitude, if we consider that here we are in some measure prepared for the glory of the heavenly kingdom. For the Lord has
ordained, that they who are to be hereafter crowned in heaven,
must first engage in conflicts on earth, that they may not triumph
without having surmounted the difficulties of warfare and obtained
the victory. Another reason is, that here we begin in various blessings to taste the sweetness of the Divine benignity, that our hope
and desire may be excited after the full revelation of it. When
we have come to this conclusion, that our life in this world is a
gift of the Divine clemency, which, as we owe to him, we ought to
remember with gratitude, it will then be time for us to descend to
a consideration of its most miserable condition, that we may be
delivered from excessive love of it, to which, as has been observed,
we are naturally inclined. . . .

It should be the object of believers . . . in judging of this   III. ix. 4
mortal life, that understanding it to be of itself nothing but misery,
they may apply themselves wholly, with increasing cheerfulness
and readiness, to meditate on the future and eternal life. . . . For
if heaven is our country, what is the earth but a place of exile? If
the departure out of the world is an entrance into life, what is the
world but a sepulchre? What is a continuance in it but an ab-
sorption in death? If deliverance from the body is an introduction
into complete liberty, what is the body but a prison? If to enjoy
the presence of God is the summit of felicity, is it not misery to be
destitute of it? . . . The terrestrial life . . . certainly is never to
be hated, except in as much as it keeps us obnoxious to sin; although even that hatred is not properly to be applied to life itself.
It becomes us, however, to be so affected with weariness or hatred
of it, as to desire its end, but to be also prepared to remain in it
during the Divine pleasure; that is to say, our weariness should
be remote from all murmuring and impatience. For it is a post at

III. ix. 5   which the Lord has placed us, to be retained by us till he call us away. . . . But it is monstrous, that instead of this desire of death, multitudes who boast themselves to be Christians, are filled with such a dread of it, that they tremble whenever it is mentioned, as if it were the greatest calamity that could befall them. . . . It is intolerable that there should not be in a Christian breast sufficient light of piety to overcome and suppress all that fear with superior consolation. . . . This we may positively conclude, that no man has made any good proficiency in the school of Christ, but he who joyfully expects both the day of death and that of the final resurrection. . . .

(4) RULES FOR CHRISTIAN LIVING

III. x. 2   It must be laid down as a principle, that the use of the gifts of God is not erroneous, when it is directed to the same end for which the Creator himself has created and appointed them for us; since he has created them for our benefit, not for our injury. . . . But shall the Lord have endued flowers with such beauty, to present itself to our eyes, with such sweetness of smell, to impress our sense of smelling; and shall it be unlawful for our eyes to be affected with the beautiful sight, or our olfactory nerves with the agreeable odour? What! has he not made such a distinction of colours as to render some more agreeable than others? Has he not given to gold and silver, to ivory and marble, a beauty which makes them more precious than other metals or stones? In a word, has he not made many things worthy of our estimation, independently of any nec-

III. x. 3   essary use? Let us discard, therefore, that inhuman philosophy which, allowing no use of the creatures but what is absolutely necessary, not only malignantly deprives us of the lawful enjoyment of the Divine beneficence, but which cannot be embraced till it has despoiled man of all his senses, and reduced him to a senseless block. But, on the other hand we must, with equal diligence, oppose the licentiousness of the flesh; which, unless it be rigidly

III. x. 4   restrained, transgresses every bound. . . . Though the liberty of believers in external things cannot be reduced to certain rules, yet it is evidently subject to this law, That they should indulge

III. x. 5   themselves as little as possible. . . . [Another] rule will be, That persons whose property is small should learn to be patient under their privations, that they may not be tormented with an immoderate desire of riches. . . . The Scripture has also a thìrd rule, . . . that while all these things are given to us by the Divine goodness, and appointed for our benefit, they are, as it were, deposits intrusted to our care, of which we must one day give an account. . . . Lastly, it is to be remarked, that the Lord commands every one of us, in all the actions of life, to regard his vocation. . . . He has appointed to all their particular duties in different spheres of life. . . . Every individual's line of life . . . is, as it were, a post assigned him by the Lord, that he may not wander about in uncertainty all his days. . . . Our life, therefore, will then be best regulated, when it is directed to this mark; since no one will be impelled by his own temerity to attempt more than is compatible with his calling, because he will know that it is unlawful to transgress the bounds assigned him. He that is in obscurity will lead a private life without discontent, so as not to desert the station in which God has placed him. It will also be no small alleviation of his cares, labours, troubles, and other burdens, when a man knows that in all these things he has God for his guide. The magistrate will execute his office with greater pleasure, the father of a family will confine himself to his duty with more satisfaction, and all, in their respective spheres of life, will bear and surmount the inconveniences, cares, disappointments, and anxieties which befall them, when they shall be persuaded that every individual has his burden laid upon him by God. Hence also will arise peculiar consolation, since there will be no employment so mean and sordid' (provided we follow our vocation) as not to appear truly respectable, and be deemed highly important in the sight of God. . . .

III. x. 6

CHAPTER XVII

Justification by Faith

❧

(1) JUSTIFICATION BY FAITH DEFINED

M EN, being subject to the curse of the law, have no means left
of attaining salvation but through faith alone. . . . The substance of what I have advanced is, that Christ, being given to us
by the goodness of God, is apprehended and possessed by us by
faith, by a participation of whom we receive especially two benefits. In the first place, being by his innocence reconciled to God,
we have in heaven a propitious father instead of a judge; in the
next place, being sanctified by his Spirit, we devote ourselves to
innocence and purity of life. . . . The method of justification
has been but slightly touched, because it was necessary, first to
understand that the faith, by which alone we attain gratuitous
justification through the Divine mercy, is not unattended with
good works, and what is the nature of the good works of the saints,
in which part of this question consists. The subject of justification,
therefore, must now be fully discussed, and discussed with the
recollection that it is the principal hinge by which religion is supported. . . .

But that we may not stumble at the threshold, . . . let us first
explain the meaning of these expressions *To be justified in the
sight of God, To be justified by faith* or *by works.* He is said to be

justified in the sight of God who in the Divine judgment is reputed
righteous, and accepted on account of his righteousness. . . . He is
justified who is considered not as a sinner, but as a righteous person, and on that account stands in safety before the tribunal of God,
where all sinners are confounded and ruined. . . . Thus he must
be said, therefore, to be *justified by works,* whose life discovers such
purity and holiness, as to deserve the character of righteousness
before the throne of God; or who, by the integrity of his works,
can answer and satisfy the divine judgment. On the other hand,
he will be *justified by faith,* who, being excluded from the righteousness of works, apprehends by faith the righteousness of Christ,
invested in which, he appears, in the sight of God, not as a sinner,
but as a righteous man. Thus we simply explain justification to be
an acceptance, by which God receives us into his favour, and esteems us as righteous persons; and we say that it consists in the
remission of sins and the imputation of the righteousness of Christ.
For the confirmation of this point there are many plain testi-   III. xi. 3
monies of Scripture. In the first place, that this is the proper and
most usual signification of the word, cannot be denied. But since
it would be too tedious to collect all the passages and compare
them together, let it suffice to have suggested it to the reader; for
he will easily observe it of himself. . . .

But as many persons imagine righteousness to be composed of   III. xi. 13
faith and works, let us also prove, before we proceed, that the
righteousness of faith is so exceedingly different from that of
works, that if one be established, the other must necessarily be
subverted. . . . If, by establishing our own righteousness, we
reject the righteousness of God, then, in order to obtain the latter,
the former must doubtless be entirely renounced. . . . As long as
there remains the least particle of righteousness in our works, we
retain some cause for boasting. But if faith excludes all boasting,
the righteousness of works can by no means be associated with
the righteousness of faith. . . . Adieu, therefore, to the fanciful
notion of those who imagine a righteousness compounded of faith
and works. . . . This is the sentiment of faith, by which the sinner   III. xi. 16
comes to the enjoyment of his salvation, when he knows from the
doctrine of the gospel that he is reconciled to God; that having
obtained remission of sins, he is justified by the intervention of

the righteousness of Christ; and though regenerated by the Spirit of God, he thinks on everlasting righteousness reserved for him, not in the good works to which he devotes himself, but solely in the righteousness of Christ. . . .

III. xi. 17   It is proper to recall to remembrance the relation we have before stated between faith and the gospel; since the reason why faith is said to justify, is, that it receives and embraces the righteousness offered in the gospel. But its being offered by the gospel

III. xi. 18   absolutely excludes all consideration of works. . . . The gospel differs from the law in this respect, that it does not confine righteousness to works, but rests it entirely on the mercy of God. . . .

III. xi. 21   Now, let us examine the truth of what has been asserted in the definition, that the righteousness of faith is a reconciliation with God, which consists solely in remission of sins. . . . Sin makes a division between man and God, and turns the Divine countenance away from the sinner. Nor can it be otherwise; because it is incompatible with his righteousness to have any communion with sin. Hence the apostle teaches, that man is an enemy to God, till he be reconciled to him through Christ. (*i*) Whom, therefore, the Lord receives into fellowship, him he is said to justify; because he cannot receive any one into favour or into fellowship with himself, without making him from a sinner to be a righteous person. This, we add, is accomplished by the remission of sins. For if they, whom the Lord has reconciled to himself, be judged according to their works, they will still be found actually sinners; who, notwithstanding, must be absolved and free from sin. It appears, then, that those whom God receives, are made righteous no otherwise than as they are purified by being cleansed from all their defilements by the remission of their sins; so that such a righteousness may, in one word, be denominated a remission of sins. . . .

III. xi. 23   Hence, also, it is evident, that we obtain justification before God, solely by the intervention of the righteousness of Christ. Which is equivalent to saying, that a man is righteous, not in himself, but because the righteousness of Christ is communicated to him by imputation; and this is a point which deserves an attentive consideration. For it supersedes that idle notion, that a

---

(*i*) Rom. v. 8—10.

man is justified by faith, because faith receives the Spirit of God by whom he is made righteous; which is too repugnant to the foregoing doctrine, ever to be reconcilable to it. For he must certainly be destitute of all righteousness of his own, who is taught to seek a righteousness out of himself. . . . Our righteousness is not in ourselves, but in Christ; and . . . all our title to it rests solely on our being partakers of Christ; for in possessing him, we possess all his riches with him. . . .

Here are two things to which we must always be particularly   III. xiii. 1
attentive; to maintain the glory of the Lord unimpaired and undiminished, and to preserve in our own consciences a placid composure and serene tranquillity with regard to the Divine judgment. . . . The truth . . . is, that we never truly glory in him,   III. xiii. 2
till we have entirely renounced all glory of our own. . . . Man cannot without sacrilege arrogate to himself the least particle of righteousness, because it is so much detracted and diminished from the glory of the righteousness of God. Now, if we inquire by what   III. xiii. 3
means the conscience can obtain peace before God, we shall find no other than our reception of gratuitous righteousness from his free gift. . . .

The Scripture declares that the promises of God have no efficacy,   III. xiii. 4
unless they be embraced by the conscience with a steady confidence; and whenever there is any doubt or uncertainty, it pronounces them to be made void. Again, it asserts that they have no stability if they depend on our works. Either, therefore, we must be for ever destitute of righteousness, or our works must not come into consideration, but the ground must be occupied by faith alone, whose nature it is to open the ears and shut the eyes; that is, to be intent only on the promise, and to avert the thoughts from all human dignity or merit. . . .

Whoever they are, therefore, who pretend that we are justified   III. xiii. 5
by faith, because, being regenerated, we are righteous by living a spiritual life, they have never tasted the sweetness of grace, so as to have confidence that God would be propitious to them. . . . Believers should conclude that they cannot hope for an inheritance in the kingdom of heaven on any other foundation, but because, being ingrafted into the body of Christ, they are gratuitously accounted righteous. For with respect to justification, faith is a

thing merely passive, bringing nothing of our own to conciliate the favour of God, but receiving what we need from Christ.

(2) MAN NOT SAVED BY HIS OWN RIGHTEOUSNESS

III. xiv. 1   For the further elucidation of this subject, let us examine what kind of righteousness can be found in men during the whole course of their lives. Let us divide them into four classes. For either they are destitute of the knowledge of God, and immerged in idolatry; or, having been initiated by the sacraments, they lead impure lives, denying God in their actions, while they confess him with their lips, and belong to Christ only in name; or they are hypocrites, concealing the iniquity of their hearts with vain disguises; or, being regenerated by the Spirit of God, they devote themselves to true holiness. In the first of these classes, judged of according to their natural characters, from the crown of the head to the sole of the foot there will not be found a single III. xiv. 2   spark of goodness. . . . I do not deny, that whatever excellences appear in unbelievers, they are the gifts of God, . . . since there is nothing in any respect laudable which does not proceed from III. xiv. 3   him. Nevertheless the observation of Augustine is strictly true — that all who are strangers to the religion of the one true God, however they may be esteemed worthy of admiration for their reputed virtue, not only merit no reward, but are rather deserving of punishment, because they contaminate the pure gifts of God with the pollution of their own hearts. . . . When we remember that the end of what is right is always to serve God, whatever is directed to any other end, can have no claim to that appellation. . . . Moral duties are estimated not by external actions, but III. xiv. 4   by the ends for which such actions are designed. . . . Hence we clearly perceive that all the thoughts, meditations, and actions of man antecedent to a reconciliation to God by faith, are accursed, and not only of no avail to justification, but certainly deserving III. xiv. 5   of condemnation. . . . The Scripture invariably proclaims, that God finds nothing in men which can incite him to bless them. . . . What can a dead man do to recover life? . . . For, according to the constitution of our nature, oil might be extracted from a stone sooner than we could perform a good work. . . .

The same reasoning may be applied to the second and third III. xiv. 7
classes of men in the division stated above. For the impurity
of the conscience proves, that they are neither of them yet regenerated by the Spirit of God; and their unregeneracy betrays also their want of faith: whence it appears, that they are
not yet reconciled to God, or justified in his sight, since these
blessings are only attained by faith. . . . The greatest sinner,
as soon as he has performed two or three duties of the law, doubts
not but they are accepted of him for righteousness; but the Lord
positively denies that any sanctification is acquired by such actions, unless the heart be previously well purified. (z) . . . Let III. xiv. 8
hypocrites go now, and, retaining depravity concealed in their
hearts, endeavour by their works to merit the favour of God. But
by such means they will add provocation to provocation; for " the
sacrifice of the wicked is an abomination to the Lord; but the
prayer of the upright " alone " is his delight." (c) We lay it down,
therefore, as an undoubted truth, which ought to be well known
to such as are but moderately versed in the Scriptures, that even
the most splendid works of men not yet truly sanctified, are so
far from righteousness in the Divine view, that they are accounted
sins. . . . The works of a man do not conciliate God's favour to
his person; but, on the contrary, . . . works are never acceptable
to God, unless the person who performs them has previously
found favour in his sight. . . .

Let us now examine what degree of righteousness is possessed III. xiv. 9
by those whom we have ranked in the fourth class. We admit,
that when God, by the interposition of the righteousness of Christ,
reconciles us to himself, and having granted us the free remission of our sins, esteems us as righteous persons, to this mercy he
adds also another blessing; for he dwells in us by his Holy
Spirit, by whose power our carnal desires are daily more and
more mortified, and we are sanctified, that is, consecrated to the
Lord unto real purity of life, having our hearts moulded to obey
his law, so that it is our prevailing inclination to submit to
his will, and to promote his glory alone by all possible means.
But even while, under the guidance of the Holy Spirit, we are

---

(z) Hag. ii. 11 –14   (c) Prov. xv. 8.

walking in the ways of the Lord, — that we may not forget ourselves, and be filled with pride, we feel such remains of imperfection, as afford us abundant cause for humility. . . . In the first
place, I assert, that the best of their performances are tarnished
and corrupted by some carnal impurity and debased by a mixture
of some alloy. Let any holy servant of God select from his whole
life that which he shall conceive to have been the best of all his
actions, and let him examine it with attention on every side; he
will undoubtedly discover in it some taint of the corruption of the
flesh; since our alacrity to good actions is never what it ought to
III. xiv. 10 be, but our course is retarded by great debility. . . . In the next
place, even though it were possible for us to perform any works
completely pure and perfect, yet one sin is sufficient to extinguish
and annihilate all remembrance of antecedent righteousness. . . .
Since this mortal life is never pure or free from sin, whatever
righteousness we might acquire being perpetually corrupted, over-
powered, and destroyed by subsequent sins, it would neither be
admitted in the sight of God, nor be imputed to us for righteousness. Lastly, . . . if we seek righteousness by the law, it is in
vain for us to perform two or three works; perpetual observance
of the law is indispensably necessary. . . .

III. xiv. 11   We must strenuously insist on these two points — first, that
there never was an action performed by a pious man, which, if
examined by the scrutinizing eye of Divine justice, would not
deserve condemnation; and secondly, if any such thing be admitted, (though it cannot be the case with any individual of mankind,) yet being corrupted and contaminated by the sins, of which
its performer is confessedly guilty, it loses every claim to the
III. xv. 3   Divine favour. . . . It is beyond a doubt, that whatever is laudable in our works proceeds from the grace of God; and that we
cannot properly ascribe the least portion of it to ourselves. If we
truly and seriously acknowledge this truth, not only all confidence,
but likewise all idea of merit, immediately vanishes. . . . Good
works . . . are pleasing to God, and not unprofitable to the
authors of them; and they will moreover receive the most ample
blessings from God as their reward; not because they merit them,
but because the Divine goodness has freely appointed them this
reward. . . .

(3) COMMON OBJECTIONS TO JUSTIFICATION
BY FAITH ANSWERED

Some impious persons . . . accuse us, in the first place, of **III. xvi. 1**
destroying good works, and seducing men from the pursuit of
them, when we say that they are not justified by works, nor saved
through their own merit; and secondly, of making too easy a road
to righteousness, when we teach that it consists in the gratuitous
remission of sins; and of enticing men, by this allurement, to the
practice of sin, to which they have naturally too strong a propensity. . . . I will briefly reply to . . . both . . . these calumnies. . . . We never dream either of a faith destitute of good
works, or of a justification unattended by them: this is the sole
difference, that while we acknowledge a necessary connection between faith and good works, we attribute justification, not to works,
but to faith. Our reason for this we can readily explain, if we
only turn to Christ, towards whom faith is directed, and from
whom it receives all its virtue. Why, then, are we justified by
faith? Because by faith we apprehend the righteousness of Christ,
which is the only medium of our reconciliation to God. But this
you cannot attain, without at the same time attaining to sanctification; for he " is made unto us wisdom and righteousness, and
sanctification and redemption." (z) Christ therefore justifies no
one whom he does not also sanctify. For these benefits are perpetually and indissolubly connected, so that whom he illuminates
with his wisdom, them he redeems; whom he redeems, he justifies; whom he justifies, he sanctifies. . . . Thus we see how true
it is that we are justified, not without works, yet not by works;
since union with Christ, by which we are justified, contains sanctification as well as righteousness.

It is also exceedingly false, that the minds of men are seduced **III. xvi. 2**
from an inclination to virtue, by our divesting them of all ideas
of merit. . . . When they say that there will be no concern about
the proper regulation of our life without a hope of reward being
proposed, they altogether deceive themselves. If they only mean
that men serve God in expectation of a reward, and hire or sell

---

(z) 1 Cor. i. 30.

their services to him, they gain but little; for he will be freely worshipped and freely loved, and he approves of that worshipper who, after being deprived of all hope of receiving any reward, still ceases not to worship him. . . .

III. xvi. 4   But the most futile of all their calumnies is, that men are encouraged to the practice of sin by our maintaining the gratuitous remission of sins, in which we make righteousness to consist. For we say that so great a blessing could never be compensated by any virtue of ours, and that therefore it could never be obtained, unless it were gratuitously bestowed; moreover, that it is gratuitous to us indeed, but not so to Christ, whom it cost so much, even his own most sacred blood, beside which no price sufficiently valuable could be paid to Divine justice. . . . Must not persons who hear these things conceive a greater horror of sin, than if it were said to be cleansed by a sprinkling of good works? And if they have any fear of God, will they not dread, after being once purified, to plunge themselves again into the mire, and thereby to disturb and infect, as far as they can, the purity of this fountain? . . . They say, that righteousness, if it ever be defective, is restored and repaired by works of satisfaction. We think it so valuable that no compensation of works can be adequate to it; and therefore that for its restitution we must have recourse to the mercy of God alone. . . .

III. xvii. 1   But since they assail us besides . . . with other weapons, let us also proceed to the repulsion of them. In the first place, they return to the legal promises which the Lord gave to the observers of his law, and inquire whether we suppose them to be entirely vain, or of any validity. As it would be harsh and ridiculous to say they are vain, they take it for granted that they have some efficacy. Hence they argue, that we are not justified by faith alone. . . . We have already shown how, if we adhere to the law, being destitute of every blessing, we are obnoxious to the curse which is denounced on all transgressors. For the Lord promises nothing, except to the perfect observers of his law, of which description not one can be found. The consequence then is, that all mankind are proved by the law to be obnoxious to the curse and wrath of God; in order to be saved from which, they need deliverance from the power of the law, and emancipation from its servitude; not a carnal liberty, which would seduce us from obedience to the law, invite to all kinds of licentiousness, break down the barriers of inordinate desire, and give the reins to every lawless passion; but a spiritual liberty, which will console and elevate a distressed and dejected conscience, showing it to be delivered from the curse and condemnation under which it was held by the law. This liberation from subjection to the law, and manumission, (if I may use the term,) we attain, when we apprehend by faith the mercy of God in Christ, by which we are assured of the remission of sins, by the sense of which the law penetrated us with compunction and remorse. For this reason all the promises of the law would be ineffectual and vain, unless we were assisted by the goodness of God in the gospel. For the condition of a perfect obedience to the law, on which they depend, and in consequence of which alone they are to be fulfilled, will never be performed. Now, the Lord affords this assistance, not by leaving a part of righteousness in our works, and supplying part from his mercy, but by appointing Christ alone for the completion of righteousness. . . .   III. xvii. 2

Let us now proceed to those passages which affirm that "God will render to every man according to his deeds;" (f) that "every one may receive the things done in his body, according to that he hath done, whether it be good or bad." (g) "Tribulation and anguish upon every soul that doeth evil; but glory, honour, and peace, to every man that worketh good." (h) . . . And with these let us also connect those which represent eternal life as the reward of works, such as the following: "The recompense of a man's hands shall be rendered unto him." (l) "He that feareth the commandment shall be rewarded." (m) "Rejoice and be exceeding glad; for great is your reward in heaven." (n) "Every one shall receive his own reward, according to his own labour." (o) The declaration, that God will render to every one according to his works, is easily explained. For that phrase indicates the order of events, rather than the cause of them. . . . Though [the Lord] . . . receives his children into eternal life,   III. xviii. 1

(f) Rom. ii. 6.   Matt. xvi. 27.   (g) 2 Cor. v. 10.   (h) Rom. ii. 9, 10.
   (l) Prov. xii. 14.   (m) Prov. xiii. 13.
   (n) Matt. v. 12.   Luke vi. 23.   (o) 1 Cor. iii. 8.

. . . of his mere mercy, yet since he conducts them to the possession of it through a course of good works, that he may fulfil his
work in them in the order he has appointed, we need not wonder
if they are said to be rewarded according to their works, by which
they are undoubtedly prepared to receive the crown of immortality. . . .

III. xviii. 2   We have no reason to infer from the term *reward*, that good
works are the cause of salvation. . . . Let this truth be established
in our minds, that the kingdom of heaven is not the stipend of
servants, but the inheritance of children, which will be enjoyed
only by those whom the Lord adopts as his children, and for no
other cause than on account of this adoption. . . .

III. xviii. 4   There is no objection against our following the example of
the Scripture in calling eternal life *a reward;* since in that state
the Lord receives his people from labor into rest; from affliction
into prosperity and happiness; from sorrow into joy; from
poverty into affluence; from ignominy into glory; and commutes
all the evils which they have endured for blessings of superior
magnitude. So, likewise, it will occasion no inconvenience, if we
consider holiness of life as the way, not which procures our admission into the glory of the heavenly kingdom, but through
which the elect are conducted by their God to the manifestation
of it; since it is his good pleasure to glorify them whom he has
sanctified. Only let us not imagine a reciprocal relation of merit
and reward. . . . Nothing is clearer, than that the promise of a
reward to good works is designed to afford some consolation to
the weakness of our flesh, but not to inflate our minds with vain-
glory. Whoever, therefore, infers from this, that there is any merit
in works, or balances the work against the reward, errs very widely
from the true design of God. . . .

(4) JUSTIFICATION BY FAITH AND CHRISTIAN LIBERTY

III. xix. 1   We have now to treat of Christian liberty, . . . a subject of the
first importance. . . . It is an appendix to justification, and affords no small assistance towards the knowledge of its influence.
. . . For some, under the pretext of this liberty, cast off all obedi-

ence to God, and precipitate themselves into the most unbridled licentiousness; and some despise it, supposing it to be subversive of all moderation, order, and moral distinctions. . . .

Christian liberty, according to my judgment, consists of three parts. The first part is, that the consciences of believers, when seeking an assurance of their justification before God, should raise themselves above the law, and forget all the righteousness of the law. . . . The whole life of Christians ought to be an exercise of piety, since they are called to sanctification. (*f*) It is the office of the law to remind them of their duty, and thereby to excite them to the pursuit of holiness and integrity. But when their consciences are solicitous how God may be propitiated, what answer they shall make, and on what they shall rest their confidence, if called to his tribunal, there must then be no consideration of the requisitions of the law, but Christ alone must be proposed for righteousness, who exceeds all the perfection of the law. . . . III. xix. 2

The second part of Christian liberty, which is dependent on the first, is, that their consciences do not observe the law, as being under any legal obligations; but that, being liberated from the yoke of the law, they yield a voluntary obedience to the will of God. . . . They who are bound by the yoke of the law, are like slaves who have certain daily tasks appointed by their masters. . . . But children, who are treated by their parents in a more liberal manner, hesitate not to present to them their imperfect, and in some respects faulty works, in confidence that their obedience and promptitude of mind will be accepted by them, though they have not performed all that they wished. Such children ought we to be, feeling a certain confidence that our services, however small, rude, and imperfect, will be approved by our most indulgent Father. . . . III. xix. 4 III. xix. 5

The third part of Christian liberty teaches us, that we are bound by no obligation before God respecting external things, which in themselves are indifferent; but that we may indifferently sometimes use, and at other times omit them. And the knowledge of this liberty also is very necessary for us; for without it we III. xix. 7

(*f*) Ephes. i. 4. 1 Thess. iv. 3, 7.

shall have no tranquillity of conscience, nor will there be any end of superstitions. . . . Some are hurried by despair into a vortex of confusion, from which they see no way of escape; and some, despising God, and casting off all fear of him, make a way of ruin for themselves. . . .

III. xix. 11   I shall now . . . make some observations concerning offences. . . . I approve of the common distinction between an offence given and an offence taken. . . . An offence is always said to be given in any action, the fault of which proceeds from the performer of that action. An offence taken is, when any transaction, not otherwise unseasonable or culpable, is, through malevolence, or some perverse disposition, construed into an occasion of offence. . . . The first species of offence affects none but the weak; the second is created by moroseness of temper, and Pharisaical superciliousness. . . . We shall so temper the use of our liberty, that it ought to submit to the ignorance of weak brethren, but not at all to the austerity of Pharisees. . . . Our liberty is not given us to be used in opposition to our weak neighbours, to whom charity obliges us to do every possible service; but rather in order that, having peace with God in our minds, we may also live peaceably among men. But how much attention should be paid to an offence taken by Pharisees, we learn from our Lord's injunction, "Let them alone; they be blind leaders of the blind." (z) . . .

III. xix. 12   Nothing can be plainer than this rule, that our liberty should be used, if it conduces to our neighbour's edification; but that if it be not beneficial to our neighbour, it should be abridged.

III. xix. 13   . . . But whatever I have advanced respecting the avoidance of offences, I wish to be referred to indifferent and unimportant things; for necessary duties must not be omitted through fear of any offence: as our liberty should be subject to charity, so charity itself ought to be subservient to the purity of faith. . . .

III. xix. 14   Now, since the consciences of believers . . . have been delivered by the favour of Christ from all necessary obligation to the observance of those things in which the Lord has been pleased they should be left free, we conclude that they are exempt from

III. xix. 15   all human authority. . . . Man is under two kinds of government

---

(z) Matt. xv. 14.

— one spiritual, by which the conscience is formed to piety and the service of God; the other political, by which a man is instructed in the duties of humanity and civility, which are to be observed in an intercourse with mankind. They are generally, and not improperly, denominated the spiritual and the temporal jurisdiction. . . . The question, which, as I have observed, is in itself not very obscure or intricate, greatly perplexes many, because they do not distinguish with sufficient precision between the external jurisdiction and the court of conscience. . . .

CHAPTER XVIII

Prayer, the Principal Exercise of Faith

(1) THE NECESSITY FOR PRAYER

III. xx. 1 FROM the subjects already discussed, we clearly perceive how utterly destitute man is of every good, and in want of all the means of salvation. Wherefore, if he seek for relief in his necessities, he must go out of himself, and obtain it from some other quarter. . . . Since we have been taught by faith to acknowledge, that whatever we want for the supply of our necessities is in God and our Lord Jesus Christ, in whom it has pleased the Father all the fulness of his bounty should dwell, that we may all draw from it, as from a most copious fountain, it remains for us to seek in him, and by prayers to implore of him, that which we have been informed resides in him. . . .

III. xx. 2 Between God and men there is a certain communication. . . . Nothing is revealed to us, to be expected from the Lord, for which we are not likewise enjoined to pray. . . . It is certainly not without reason that our heavenly Father declares, that the only fortress of salvation consists in invocation of his name; by which we call to our aid the presence of his providence, which watches over all our concerns; of his power, which supports us when

weak and ready to faint; and of his goodness, which receives us
into favour, though miserably burdened with sins; in which,
finally, we call upon him to manifest his presence with us in all
his attributes. . . .

But some will say, Does he not, without information, know   III. xx. 3
both our troubles and our necessities; so that it may appear unnecessary to solicit him with our prayers, as if he were inattentive or sleeping, till aroused by our voice? But such reasoners
advert not to the Lord's end in teaching his people to pray; for
he has appointed it not so much for his own sake as for ours. . . .
The greater the confidence . . . with which the ancient saints
gloried in the Divine benefits to themselves and others, with so
much the more earnestness were they incited to pray. . . .

(2) THE PREREQUISITES OF PRAYER

Now, for conducting prayer in a right and proper manner, the   III. xx. 4
first rule is, that our heart and mind be composed to a suitable
frame, becoming those who enter into conversation with God. . . .
I maintain the necessity of dismissing all foreign and external
cares, by which the wandering mind may be hurried hither and
thither, and dragged from heaven down to earth. . . . Both these   III. xx. 5
things are highly worthy of observation — first, that whoever
engages in prayer, should apply all his faculties and attention
to it, and not be distracted. . . . Our second proposition is, that
we must pray for no more than God permits. For though he enjoins us to pour out our hearts before him, (f) yet he does not
carelessly give the reins to affections of folly and depravity. . . .

Let this be the second rule: That in our supplications we should   III. xx. 6
have a real and permanent sense of our indigence, and seriously
considering our necessity of all that we ask, should join with
the petitions themselves a serious and ardent desire of obtaining
them. For multitudes carelessly recite a form of prayer, as though
they were discharging a task imposed on them by God; . . .
none pray aright, and . . . no others are heard, but the sincere   III. xx. 7
worshippers of God. . . .

(f) Psalm lxii. 8.

III. xx. 8   To these must be added a third rule — That whoever presents himself before God for the purpose of praying to him, must renounce every idea of his own glory, reject all opinion of his own merit, and, in a word, relinquish all confidence in himself, giving, by this humiliation of himself, all the glory entirely to God; lest, arrogating any thing, though ever so little, to ourselves, we perish from his presence in consequence of our vanity. . . . The most eminent for holiness feel the greatest consternation on

III. xx. 9   entering into the presence of the Lord. . . . The commencement and even introduction to praying rightly is a supplication for pardon with an humble and ingenuous confession of guilt. . . .

III. xx. 11   The fourth and last rule is, That thus prostrate with true humility, we should nevertheless be animated to pray by the certain hope of obtaining our requests. . . . God is highly incensed by our distrust, if we supplicate him for blessings which we have no expectation of receiving. There is nothing, therefore, more suitable to the nature of prayers, than that they be conformed to this rule — not to rush forward with temerity, but to follow the steps of faith. . . .

(3) CHRIST AND PRAYER

III. xx. 17   But since there is no one of the human race worthy to present himself to God, and to enter into his presence, our heavenly Father himself, to deliver us at once from shame and fear, which might justly depress all our minds, has given us his Son Jesus Christ our Lord to be our Advocate and Mediator with him; (c) introduced by whom we may boldly approach him, confident, with such an Intercessor, that nothing we ask in his name will be

III. xx. 19   denied us. . . . Moreover, since he is the only way of access by which we are permitted to approach God, to them who deviate from this road, and desert this entrance, there remains no other way of access to God, nor any thing on his throne but wrath, judg-

III. xx. 21   ment, and terror. . . . With respect to the saints who are dead in the flesh, but live in Christ, if we attribute any intercession to them, let us not imagine that they have any other way of praying

_____

(c) 1 Tim. ii. 5. 1 John ii. 1.

to God than by Christ, who is the only way, or that their prayers
are accepted by God in any other name. . . .

Diligence in prayer, although it chiefly respects the particular   III. xx. 29
and private devotions of each individual, has, notwithstanding,
some reference also to the public prayers of the Church. . . .
Certain hours are fixed and prescribed, though indifferent with
God, yet necessary to the customs of men, that the benefit of all
may be regarded, and all the affairs of the Church be administered.
. . . We must learn not only a certain rule, but also the form of   III. xx. 34
praying; even that which our heavenly Father has given us by his
beloved Son. (n) . . . This form or rule of prayer, whichever   III. xx. 35
appellation be given to it, is composed of six petitions. . . .
Though the whole prayer is such, that in every part of it the principal regard must be paid to the glory of God, yet to this the first
three petitions are particularly devoted, and to this alone we
ought to attend in them, without any consideration of our own
interest. The remaining three concern ourselves, and are expressly
assigned to supplications for those things which tend to our
benefit. . . . Whatever we ought, or are even at liberty, to seek   III. xx. 48
from God, is stated to us in this model and directory for prayer,
given by that best of masters, Christ, whom the Father has set
over us as our Teacher, and to whom alone he has enjoined us to
listen. (b) . . .

We ought every one of us, for the sake of regularity, to appoint   III. xx. 50
particular hours which should not elapse without prayer, and
which should witness all the affections of the mind entirely engaged in this exercise; as, when we rise in the morning, before
we enter on the business of the day, when we sit down to meat,
when we have been fed by the Divine blessing, when we retire to
rest. This must not be a superstitious observance of hours, by
which, as if discharging our debt to God, we may fancy ourselves
discharged from all obligation for the remaining hours; but a
discipline for our weakness, which may thus, from time to time,
be exercised and stimulated. . . . If, with minds composed to this   III. xx. 51
obedience, we suffer ourselves to be governed by the laws of Divine
Providence, we shall easily learn to persevere in prayer, and with

---

(n) Matt. vi. 9. Luke xi. 2.   (b) Matt. xvii. 5.

suspended desires to wait patiently for the Lord; assured, though he does not discover himself, yet that he is always near us, and in his own time will declare that his ears have not been deaf to those prayers which, to human apprehension, seemed to be neglected. . . .

CHAPTER XIX

The Doctrine of Election

❧

(1) THE DOCTRINE STATED, DIFFICULTIES INVOLVED

IF IT be evidently the result of the Divine will, that salvation is III. xxi. 1 freely offered to some, and others are prevented from attaining it, — this immediately gives rise to important and difficult questions, which are incapable of any other explication, than by the establishment of pious minds in what ought to be received concerning election and predestination — a question, in the opinion of many, full of perplexity; for they consider nothing more unreasonable, than that, of the common mass of mankind, some should be predestinated to salvation, and others to destruction. . . . We shall never be clearly convinced as we ought to be, that our salvation flows from the fountain of God's free mercy, till we are acquainted with his eternal election, which illustrates the grace of God by this comparison, that he adopts not all promiscuously to the hope of salvation, but gives to some what he refuses to others. . . .

Before I enter on the subject itself, I must address some preliminary observations to two sorts of persons. The discussion of predestination — a subject of itself rather intricate — is made very perplexed, and therefore dangerous, by human curiosity, which no barriers can restrain from wandering into forbidden labyrinths, and soaring beyond its sphere, as if determined to leave none of the Divine secrets unscrutinized or unexplored. . . .

III. xxi. 2   Let us, then, in the first place, bear in mind, that to desire any other knowledge of predestination than what is unfolded in the word of God, indicates as great folly, as a wish to walk through unpassable roads, or to see in the dark. Nor let us be ashamed to be ignorant of some things relative to a subject in which there

III. xxi. 3   is a kind of learned ignorance. . . . Others, desirous of remedying this evil, will have all mention of predestination to be as it were buried; they teach men to avoid every question concerning it as they would a precipice. . . . To observe, therefore, the legitimate boundary on this side also, we must recur to the word of the Lord, which affords a certain rule for the understanding. For the Scripture is the school of the Holy Spirit, in which, as nothing necessary and useful to be known is omitted, so nothing is taught which it is not beneficial to know. Whatever, therefore, is declared in the Scripture concerning predestination, we must be cautious not to withhold from believers, lest we appear either to defraud them of the favor of their God, or to reprove and censure the Holy Spirit for publishing what it would be useful by any means

III. xxi. 4   to suppress. . . . We should neither scrutinize those things which the Lord has left concealed, nor neglect those which he has openly exhibited, lest we be condemned for excessive curiosity on the one hand, or for ingratitude on the other. . . .

III. xxi. 5   Predestination, by which God adopts some to the hope of life, and adjudges others to eternal death, . . . is involved in many cavils, especially by those who make foreknowledge the cause of it. We maintain, that both belong to God; but it is preposterous to represent one as dependent on the other. When we attribute foreknowledge to God, we mean that all things have ever been, and perpetually remain, before his eyes, so that to his knowledge nothing is future or past, but all things are present; and present in such a manner, that he does not merely conceive of them from ideas formed in his mind, as things remembered by us appear present to our minds, but really beholds and sees them as if actually placed before him. . . . Predestination we call the eternal decree of God, by which he has determined in himself, what he would have to become of every individual of mankind. For they are not all created with a similar destiny; but eternal life is foreordained for some, and eternal damnation for others. Every man, therefore, being created for one or the other of these ends, we say, he is predestinated either to life or to death. This God has not only testified in particular persons, but has given a specimen of it in the whole posterity of Abraham. . . .

In conformity . . . to the clear doctrine of the Scripture, we **III. xxi. 7** assert, that by an eternal and immutable counsel, God has once for all determined, both whom he would admit to salvation, and whom he would condemn to destruction. We affirm that this counsel, as far as concerns the elect, is founded on his gratuitous mercy, totally irrespective of human merit; but that to those whom he devotes to condemnation, the gate of life is closed by a just and irreprehensible, but incomprehensible, judgment. In the elect, we consider calling as an evidence of election, and justification as another token of its manifestation, till they arrive in glory, which constitutes its completion. As God seals his elect by vocation and justification, so by excluding the reprobate from the knowledge of his name and the sanctification of his Spirit, he affords an indication of the judgment that awaits them. . . .

(2) SCRIPTURAL BASIS OF ELECTION

It is a notion commonly entertained, that God, foreseeing what **III. xxii. 1** would be the respective merits of every individual, makes a correspondent distinction between different persons; that he adopts as his children such as he foreknows will be deserving of his grace, and devotes to the damnation of death others, whose dispositions he sees will be inclined to wickedness and impiety. . . . God's sovereign election of some, and preterition of others, they make the subject of formal accusation against him. . . . Now, it is of importance to attend to what the Scripture declares respecting every individual. Paul's assertion, that we were " chosen in Christ before the foundation of the world," (g) certainly precludes any consideration of merit in us; for it is as though he had said, our

---

(g) Ephes. i. 4.

heavenly Father, finding nothing worthy of his choice in all the posterity of Adam, turned his views towards his Christ, to choose members from his body whom he would admit to the fellowship of life. Let believers, then, be satisfied with this reason, that we were adopted in Christ to the heavenly inheritance, because in ourselves we were incapable of such high dignity. . . .

III. xxii. 3   If [God] . . . chose us that we should be holy, his foresight of our future holiness was not the cause of his choice. For these two propositions, That the holiness of believers is the fruit of election, and, That they attain it by means of works, are incompatible with each other. Nor is there any force in the cavil to which they frequently resort, that the grace of election was not God's reward of antecedent works, but his gift to future ones. For when it is said, that believers were elected that they should be holy, it is fully implied, that the holiness they were in future to possess had its origin in election. . . .

III. xxii. 7   Let the supreme Master and Judge decide the whole matter. Beholding in his hearers such extreme obduracy, that his discourses were scattered among the multitude almost without any effect, to obviate this offence, he exclaims, " All that the Father giveth me, shall come to me. And this is the Father's will, that of all which he hath given me, I should lose nothing." (y) Observe, the origin is from the donation of the Father, that we are given into the custody and protection of Christ. . . . The language of Christ is too clear to be perplexed by the quibbles of sophistry: "No man can come to me, except the Father draw him. Every man that hath heard and learned of the Father, cometh unto me." (z) . . . It must be admitted, that when Christ asserts his knowledge of whom he has chosen, it refers to a particular class of mankind, and that they are distinguished, not by the nature of their virtues, but by the decree of Heaven. Whence it follows, that none attain any excellence by their own ability or industry, since Christ represents himself as the author of election. . . . The conclusion is, that God creates whom he chooses to be his children by gratuitous adoption; that the cause of this is wholly in himself; because he exclusively regards his own secret determination. . . .

(y) John vi. 37, 39.   (z) John vi. 44, 45.

It is objected by some, that God will be inconsistent with himself, if he invites all men universally to come to him, and receives only a few elect, . . . that by external preaching all are called to repentance and faith, and yet that the spirit of repentance and faith is not given to all. . . . What they assume, I deny as being false in two respects. For he who threatens drought to one city while it rains upon another, and who denounces to another place a famine of doctrine, (*f*) lays himself under no positive obligation to call all men alike. And he who, forbidding Paul to preach the word in Asia, and suffering him not to go into Bithynia, calls him into Macedonia, (*g*) demonstrates his right to distribute this treasure to whom he pleases. In Isaiah, he still more fully declares his destination of the promises of salvation exclusively for the elect; for of them only, and not indiscriminately of all mankind, he declares that they shall be his disciples. (*h*) Whence it appears, that when the doctrine of salvation is offered to all for their effectual benefit, it is a corrupt prostitution of that which is declared to be reserved particularly for the children of the church. . . . Let this suffice, that though the voice of the gospel addresses all men generally, yet the gift of faith is bestowed on few. . . . It is no new thing for the seed to fall among thorns or in stony places; not only because most men are evidently in actual rebellion against God, but because they are not all endued with eyes and ears. Where, then, will be the consistency of God's calling to himself such as he knows will never come? . . . Faith, indeed, is properly connected with election, provided it occupies the second place. This order is clearly expressed in these words of Christ: " This is the Father's will, that of all which he hath given me, I should lose nothing. And this is the will of him that sent me, that every one which believeth on the Son, may have everlasting life." (*o*) . . .

Now, with respect to the reprobate, . . . if . . . we can assign no reason why he grants mercy to his people but because such is his pleasure, neither shall we find any other cause but his will for the reprobation of others. For when God is said to harden or

III. xxii. 10

III. xxii. 11

(*f*) Amos iv. 7; viii. 11.   (*g*) Acts xvi. 6—10.   (*h*) Isaiah viii. 16, &c.
(*o*) John vi. 39, 40.

show mercy to whom he pleases, men are taught by this declaration to seek no cause beside his will. . . .

(3) COMMON OBJECTIONS TO ELECTION ANSWERED

III. xxiii. 1 Many, indeed, as if they wished to avert odium from God, admit election in such a way as to deny that any one is reprobated. But this is puerile and absurd, because election itself could not exist without being opposed to reprobation. . . . Whom God passes by . . . he reprobates, and from no other cause than his determination to exclude them from the inheritance which he predestines for his children. . . . Now, how will those, who admit not that any are reprobated by God, evade this declaration of Christ: "Every plant which my heavenly Father hath not planted, shall be rooted up?" (y) . . . But if they cease not their clamour, let the sobriety of faith be satisfied with this admonition of Paul, that . . . God . . . endures, "with much long-suffering, the vessels of wrath fitted to destruction;" and on the other, makes "known the riches of his glory on the vessels of mercy, whom he had afore prepared unto glory." (z) . . .

III. xxiii. 2 Foolish mortals enter into many contentions with God, as though they could arraign him to plead to their accusations. In the first place they inquire, by what right the Lord is angry with his creatures who had not provoked him by any previous offence; for that to devote to destruction whom he pleases, is more like the caprice of a tyrant than the lawful sentence of a judge; that men have reason, therefore, to expostulate with God, if they are predestinated to eternal death without any demerit of their own, merely by his sovereign will. . . . The will of God is the highest rule of justice; so that what he wills must be considered just, for this very reason, because he wills it. When it is inquired, therefore, why the Lord did so, the answer must be, Because he would. . . .

III. xxiii. 3 If any one attack us with such an inquiry as this, why God has from the beginning predestinated some men to death, who, not yet being brought into existence, could not yet deserve the sentence of

---

(y) Matt. xv. 13. (z) Rom. ix. 22, 23.

death, — we will reply by asking them, in return, what they suppose God owes to man, if he chooses to judge of him from his own nature. . . . If all whom the Lord predestinates to death are in their natural condition liable to the sentence of death, what injustice do they complain of receiving from him? . . .

They further object, Were they not, by the decree of God, antecedently predestinated to that corruption which is now stated as the cause of condemnation? . . . Is he not unjust, therefore, in treating his creatures with such cruel mockery? . . . We will answer them thus in the language of Paul: " O man, who art thou that repliest against God? Shall the thing formed say to him that formed it, Why hast thou made me thus? Hath not the potter power over the clay, of the same lump, to make one vessel unto honour and another unto dishonour? " (b) . . . The apostle . . . has shown that the reason of the Divine justice is too high to be measured by a human standard, or comprehended by the littleness of the human mind. . . .

III. xxiii. 4

Impiety produces also a second objection, which directly tends, not so much to the crimination of God, as to the vindication of the sinner. . . . Why should God impute as a fault to man those things which were rendered necessary by his predestination? . . . If, by the Divine Providence, man was created in such a state as afterwards to do whatever he actually does, he ought not to be charged with guilt for things which he cannot avoid, and to which the will of God constrains him. Let us see, then, how this difficulty should be solved. In the first place, the declaration of Solomon ought to be universally admitted, that " the Lord hath made all things for himself; yea, even the wicked for the day of evil." (e) Observe; all things being at God's disposal, and the decision of salvation or death belonging to him, he orders all things by his counsel and decree in such a manner, but some men are born devoted from the womb to certain death, that his name may be glorified in their destruction. . . .

III. xxiii. 6

The reprobate wish to be thought excusable in sinning, because they cannot avoid a necessity of sinning; especially since this necessity is laid upon them by the ordination of God. But we deny

III. xxiii. 9

(b) Rom. ix. 20, 21.   (e) Prov. xvi. 4.

this to be a just excuse; because the ordination of God, by which they complain that they are destined to destruction, is guided by equity, unknown indeed to us, but indubitably certain. . . . For though, by the eternal providence of God, man was created to that misery to which he is subject, yet the ground of it he has derived from himself, not from God. . . .

III. xxiii. 10   The doctrine of God's predestination is calumniated by its adversaries, as involving a third absurdity; . . . that he is a respecter of persons, which the Scripture uniformly denies; that, therefore, either the Scripture is inconsistent with itself, or in the election of God regard is had to merits. . . . They ask how it happens, that of two persons distinguished from each other by no merit, God, in his election, leaves one and takes another. I, on the other hand, ask them, whether they suppose him that is taken to possess any thing that can attract the favour of God. If they confess that he has not, as indeed they must, it will follow, that God looks not at man, but derives his motive to favour him from his own goodness. God's election of one man, therefore, while he rejects another, proceeds not from any respect of man, but solely from his own mercy; which may freely display and exert itself wherever and whenever it pleases. . . .

III. xxiii. 12   Another argument often urged to overthrow predestination is, that its establishment would destroy all solicitude and exertion for rectitude of conduct. For who can hear, they say, that either life or death is appointed for him by God's eternal and immutable decree, without immediately concluding that it is of no importance how he conducts himself. . . . But Paul declares the end of our election to be, that we may lead a holy and blameless life. (n) If the object of election be holiness of life, it should rather awaken and stimulate us to a cheerful practice of it, than be used as a pretext for slothfulness. But how inconsistent is it to cease from the practice of virtue because election is sufficient to salvation, while the end proposed in election is our diligent performance of virtuous actions! . . .

(n) Ephes. i. 4.

(4) EFFECTUAL CALLING

In order to a further elucidation of the subject, it is necessary   III. xxiv. 1
to treat of the calling of the elect, and of the blinding and harden-
ing of the impious. . . . The discriminating election of God,
which is otherwise concealed within himself, he manifests only by
his calling, which may therefore with propriety be termed the
testification or evidence of it. " For whom he did foreknow, he
also did predestinate to be conformed to the image of his Son.
Moreover, whom he did predestinate, them he also called; and
whom he called, them he also justified," in order to their eventual
glorification. (u) Though by choosing his people, the Lord has
adopted them as his children, yet we see that they enter not on
the possession of so great a blessing till they are called; on the
other hand, as soon as they are called, they immediately enjoy
some communication of his election. . . . By connecting calling
with election, the Scripture evidently suggests that nothing is
requisite to it but the free mercy of God. For if we inquire whom
he calls, and for what reason, the answer is, those whom he had
elected. But when we come to election, we see nothing but mercy
on every side. . . .

Here two errors are to be avoided. For some suppose man to be   III. xxiv. 3
a coöperator with God, so that the validity of election depends on
his consent; thus, according to them, the will of man is superior
to the counsel of God. As though the Scripture taught, that we are
only given an ability to believe, and not faith itself. Others, not
thus enervating the grace of the Holy Spirit, yet induced by I
know not what mode of reasoning, suspend election on that which
is subsequent to it; as though it were doubtful and ineffectual till
it is confirmed by faith. That this is its confirmation *to us* is very
clear; that it is the manifestation of God's secret counsel before
concealed, we have already seen; but all that we are to understand by this, is that what was before unknown is verified, and as
it were ratified with a seal. But it is contrary to the truth to assert,
that election has no efficacy till after we have embraced the gospel,
and that this circumstance gives it all its energy. The certainty

---

(u) Rom. viii. 29, 30.

of it, indeed, we are to seek here; for if we attempt to penetrate to the eternal decree of God, we shall be ingulfed in the profound abyss. But when God has discovered it to us, we must ascend to loftier heights, that the cause may not be lost in the effect. For what can be more absurd and inconsistent, when the Scripture teaches that we are illuminated according as God has chosen us, than that our eyes should be so dazzled with the blaze of this light as to refuse to contemplate election? . . .

III. xxiv. 5   If we seek the fatherly clemency and propitious heart of God, our eyes must be directed to Christ, in whom alone the Father is well pleased. (h) If we seek salvation, life, and the immortality of the heavenly kingdom, recourse must be had to no other; for he alone is the Fountain of life, the Anchor of salvation, and the Heir of the kingdom of heaven. Now, what is the end of election, but that, being adopted as children by our heavenly Father, we may by his favour obtain salvation and immortality? . . . Christ, therefore, is the mirror, in which it behoves us to contemplate our

III. xxiv. 6   election; and here we may do it with safety. . . . If . . . we want to ascertain whether God is concerned for our salvation, let us inquire whether he has committed us to Christ, whom he con- stituted the only Saviour of all his people. Now, if we doubt whether Christ has received us into his charge and custody, he obviates this doubt, by freely offering himself as our Shepherd, and declaring that if we hear his voice, we shall be numbered among his sheep. We therefore embrace Christ, thus kindly offered to us and advancing to meet us; and he will number us with his sheep, and preserve us enclosed in his fold. . . .

III. xxiv. 7   But it daily happens, that they who appeared to belong to Christ, fall away from him again, and sink into ruin. . . . This is true; but it is equally certain, that such persons never adhered to Christ with that confidence of heart which, we say, gives us an assurance of our election. " They went out from us," says John, " but they were not of us; for if they had been of us, they would no doubt

III. xxiv. 8   have continued with us." (a) . . . The declaration of Christ, that " many are called and few chosen," is very improperly understood. For there will be no ambiguity in it, if we remember . . . that

(h) Matt. iii. 17.   (a) 1 John ii. 19.

there are two kinds of calling. For there is a universal call, by which God, in the external preaching of the word, invites all, indiscriminately, to come to him, even those to whom he intends it as a savour of death, and an occasion of heavier condemnation. There is also a special call, with which he, for the most part, favours only believers, when, by the inward illumination of his Spirit, he causes the word preached to sink into their hearts. Yet sometimes he also communicates it to those whom he only enlightens for a season, and afterwards forsakes on account of their ingratitude, and strikes with greater blindness. . . .

Now, the elect are not gathered into the fold of Christ by calling, immediately from their birth, nor all at the same time, but according as God is pleased to dispense his grace to them. Before they are gathered to that chief Shepherd, they go astray, scattered in the common wilderness, and differing in no respect from others, except in being protected by the special mercy of God from rushing down the precipice of eternal death. . . . That they go not to the most desperate extremes of impiety, is not owing to any innate goodness of theirs, but because the eye of God watches over them, and his hand is extended for their preservation. . . . Let us . . . abide by the declaration of the Scripture, that " all we like sheep have gone astray; we have turned every one to his own way," (z) that is, destruction. Those whom the Lord has determined to rescue from this gulf of perdition, he defers till his appointed season; before which he only preserves them from falling into unpardonable blasphemy.

III. xxiv. 10

III. xxiv. 11

(5) REPROBATION

As the Lord, by his effectual calling of the elect, completes the salvation to which he predestinated them in his eternal counsel, so he has his judgments against the reprobate, by which he executes his counsel respecting them. Those, therefore, whom he has created to a life of shame and a death of destruction, that they might be instruments of his wrath, and examples of his severity, he causes to reach their appointed end, sometimes depriving them

III. xxiv. 12

(z) Isaiah liii. 6.

of the opportunity of hearing the word, sometimes, by the preaching of it, increasing their blindness and stupidity. . . .

III. xxiv. 13   Why . . . in bestowing grace upon some, does he pass over others? Luke assigns a reason for the former, that they " were ordained to eternal life." What conclusion, then, shall we draw respecting the latter, but that they are vessels of wrath to dishonour? Wherefore let us not hesitate to say with Augustine, " God could convert to good the will of the wicked, because he is omnipotent. It is evident that he could. Why, then, does he not? Because he would not. Why he would not, remains with himself." For we ought not to aim at more wisdom than becomes us. . . .

III. xxiv. 14   It remains . . . to be seen why the Lord does that which it is evident he does. If it be replied, that this is done because men have deserved it by their impiety, wickedness, and ingratitude, it will be a just and true observation; but as we have not yet discovered the reason of this diversity, why some persist in obduracy while others are inclined to obedience, the discussion of it will necessarily lead us to the same remark that Paul has quoted from Moses concerning Pharaoh: " Even for this same purpose have I raised thee up, that I might show my power in thee, and that my name might be declared throughout all the earth." (h) That the reprobate obey not the word of God, when made known to them, is justly imputed to the wickedness and depravity of their hearts, provided it be at the same time stated, that they are abandoned to this depravity because they have been raised up, by a just but inscrutable judgment of God, to display his glory in their condemnation. . . . Though we cannot comprehend the reason of this, let us be content with some degree of ignorance where the wisdom of God soars into its own sublimity. . . .

III. xxiv. 17   If this be correct, it will be said there can be but little faith in the promises of the gospel, which, in declaring the will of God, assert that he wills what is repugnant to his inviolable decree. But this is far from a just conclusion. For if we turn our attention to the effect of the promises of salvation, we shall find that their universality is not at all inconsistent with the predestination of the reprobate. We know the promises to be effectual to us only when

---

(h) Rom. ix. 17.

we receive them by faith; on the contrary, the annihilation of faith
is at once an abolition of the promises. If this is their nature, we
may perceive that there is no discordance between these two things
— God's having appointed from eternity on whom he will bestow
his favour and exercise his wrath, and his proclaiming salvation
indiscriminately to all. Indeed, I maintain that there is the most
perfect harmony between them. For his sole design in thus promis-
ing, is to offer his mercy to all who desire and seek it, which none
do but those whom he has enlightened, and he enlightens all whom
he has predestinated to salvation. These persons experience the
certain and unshaken truth of the promises; so that it cannot be
pretended that there is the least contrariety between God's eternal
election and the testimony of his grace offered to believers. But
why does he mention all? It is in order that the consciences of the
pious may enjoy the more secure satisfaction, seeing that there is
no difference between sinners, provided they have faith; and, on
the other hand, that the impious may not plead the want of an
asylum to flee to from the bondage of sin, while they ungratefully
reject that which is offered to them. When the mercy of God is
offered to both by the gospel, it is faith, that is, the illumination
of God, which distinguishes between the pious and impious; so
that the former experience the efficacy of the gospel, but the latter
derive no benefit from it. Now, this illumination is regulated by
God's eternal election. . . .

[Objection is made] . . . , that nothing is more inconsistent
with the nature of God than to have two wills. This I grant . . . ,
provided it be rightly explained. . . . The solution, however, elsewhere stated by us, is fully sufficient — that though to our apprehension the will of God is manifold and various, yet he does not in
himself will things at variance with each other, but astonishes our
faculties with his various and "manifold wisdom," according to the
expression of Paul, till we shall be enabled to understand, that he
mysteriously wills what now seems contrary to his will. They im-
pertinently object, that God being the Father of all, it is unjust
for him to disinherit any but such as have previously deserved this
punishment by their own guilt. As if the goodness of God did not
extend even to dogs and swine. But if the question relates to the
human race, let them answer why God allied himself to one people

as their Father; why he gathered even from them but a very small number, as the flower of them. . . .

[Objection is made further] . . . , that God hates nothing he has made; which though I grant . . . , the doctrine I maintain still remains unshaken, that the reprobate are hated by God, and that most justly, because, being destitute of his Spirit, they can do nothing but what is deserving of his curse. They further allege, that there is no difference between the Jew and the Gentile, and therefore that the grace of God is offered indiscriminately to all: I grant it; only let them admit, according to the declaration of Paul, that God calls whom he pleases, both of the Jews and of the Gentiles, (e) so that he is under no obligations to any. In this way also we answer their arguments from another text, which says, that " God hath concluded them all in unbelief, that he might have mercy upon all; " (f) which imports that he will have the salvation of all who are saved ascribed to his mercy, though this blessing is not common to all. Now, while many arguments are advanced on both sides, let our conclusion be to stand astonished with Paul at so great a mystery, and amidst the clamour of petulant tongues let us not be ashamed of exclaiming with him, " O man, who art thou that repliest against God? " For, as Augustine justly contends, it is acting a most perverse part, to set up the measure of human justice as the standard by which to measure the justice of God. . . .

(e) Rom. ix. 24.   (f) Rom..xi. 32.

CHAPTER XX

Eschatology

❧

(1) IMMORTALITY AND THE RESURRECTION

ALL that has hitherto been stated . . . concerning our salva- III. xxv. 1
tion, requires minds elevated towards heaven, that, according to
the suggestion of Peter, we may love Christ, whom we have not
seen, and, believing in him, may " rejoice with joy unspeakable
and full of glory," till we receive " the end of our faith." (*q*) . . .
He alone . . . has made a solid proficiency in the gospel who has
been accustomed to continual meditation on the blessed resurrection. . . .

Let the importance of the object sharpen our pursuit. Paul III. xxv. 3
justly argues, that " if there be no resurrection of the dead," the
whole gospel is vain and fallacious; for we should be " of all men
the most miserable," being exposed to the hatred and reproaches
of mankind, " standing in jeopardy every hour," (*a*) and being
even like sheep destined to the slaughter; and therefore its authority would fall to the ground not in one point only, but in every
thing it contains relating to adoption and the accomplishment of
our salvation. To this subject, the most important of all, let us
give an attention never to be wearied by length of time. With this
view I have deferred what I shall briefly say of it to this place, that

---

(*q*) 1 Peter i. 8, 9.   (*a*) 1 Cor. xv. 13, &c.

the reader, after receiving Christ as the Author of complete salvation, may learn to soar higher, and may know that he is invested
with heavenly glory and immortality, in order that the whole body
may be conformed to the Head; as in his person the Holy Spirit
frequently gives an example of the resurrection. It is a thing difficult to be believed, that bodies, after having been consumed by
corruption, shall at length, at the appointed time, be raised again.
Therefore, while many of the philosophers asserted the immortality of the soul, the resurrection of the body was admitted by
few. And though this furnishes no excuse, yet it admonishes us
that this truth is too difficult to command the assent of the human
mind. To enable faith to surmount so great an obstacle, the Scripture supplies us with two assistances: one consists in the similitude
of Christ, the other in the omnipotence of God. Now, whenever the
resurrection is mentioned, let us set before us the image of Christ,
who, in our nature, which he assumed, finished his course in this
mortal life in such a manner, that, having now obtained immortality, he is the pledge of future resurrection to us. . . . Christ
. . . rose again, that we might be the companions of his future
life. He was raised by the Father, inasmuch as he was the Head
of the church, from which he does not suffer him to be separated.
He was raised by the power of the Spirit, who is given to us also
for the purpose of quickening us. In a word, he was raised that
he might be " the resurrection and the life." But as we have observed that this mirror exhibits to us a lively image of our resurrection, so it will furnish a firm foundation for our minds to rest
upon, provided we are not wearied or disturbed by the long delay;
because it is not ours to measure the moments of time by our own
inclination, but to wait patiently for God's establishment of his
kingdom in his own appointed time. . . .

III. xxv. 4   The remark we have made, that in proving the resurrection, our
minds should be directed to the infinite power of God, is briefly
suggested in these words of Paul: " Who shall change our vile
body, that it may be fashioned like unto his glorious body, according to the working whereby he is able even to subdue all things
unto himself." (p) . . . Let us remember, that no man will be

---

(p) Phil. iii. 21.

truly persuaded of the future resurrection, but he who is filled
with admiration. and ascribes to the power of God the glory that
is due to it. . . .

(2) SOME COMMON OBJECTIONS ANSWERED

Now, though the minds of men ought to be continually occupied   III. xxv. 5
with the study of this subject, yet as if they expressly intended to
abolish all remembrance of the resurrection, they have called
death the end of all things, and the destruction of man. . . . This
brutish stupidity has infected all ages of the world, and even
forced its way into the Church; for the Sadducees had the audacity publicly to profess, that there is no resurrection, and that
souls are mortal. But that none might be excused by this gross
ignorance, the very instinct of nature has always set before the eyes
of unbelievers an image of the resurrection. For what is the sacred
and inviolable custom of interring the dead, but a pledge of another life? . . .

But Satan has not only stupefied men's minds, to make them
bury the memory of the resurrection together with the bodies of
the dead, but has endeavoured to corrupt this point of doctrine by
various fictions, with an ultimate view to its total subversion.
Not to mention that he began to oppose it in the days of Paul,
not long after arose the Millenarians, who limited the reign of
Christ to a thousand years. Their fiction is too puerile to require
or deserve refutation. Nor does the Revelation, which they quote
in favour of their error, afford them any support; for the term of a
thousand years, there mentioned, (c) refers not to the eternal
blessedness of the Church, but to the various agitations which
awaited the Church in its militant state upon earth. But the whole
Scripture proclaims that there will be no end of the happiness of
the elect, or the punishment of the reprobate. Now, all those things
which are invisible to our eyes, or far above the comprehension of
our minds, must either be believed on the authority of the oracles
of God, or entirely rejected. Those who assign the children of

---

(c) Rev. xx. 4.

God a thousand years to enjoy the inheritance of the future life, little think what dishonour they cast on Christ and his kingdom. For if they are not invested with immortality, neither is Christ himself, into the likeness of whose glory they will be transformed, received up into immortal glory. If their happiness will have any end, it follows that the kingdom of Christ, on the stability of which it rests, is temporary. Lastly, these persons are extremely ignorant of all Divine things, or they are striving, with malignant perverseness, to overturn all the grace of God and power of Christ; and these can never be perfectly fulfilled till sin is abolished, and death swallowed up, and eternal life completely established. . . .

III. xxv. 6   Beside these wild notions, the perverse curiosity of man has introduced two others. Some have supposed that the whole man dies, and that souls are raised again together with bodies; others, admitting the immortality of souls, suppose they will be clothed with new bodies, and thereby deny the resurrection of the flesh. . . . It is a brutish error, to represent the spirit, formed after the image of God, as a fleeting breath which animates the body only during this perishable life, and to annihilate the temple of the Holy Spirit; in short, to despoil that part of us in which Divinity is eminently displayed, and the characters of immortality are conspicuous, of this property; so that the condition of the body must be better and more excellent than that of the soul. Very different is the doctrine of Scripture, which compares the body to a habitation, from which we depart at death; because it estimates us by that part of our nature which constitutes the distinction between us and the brutes. . . . Unless our souls survive our bodies, what is it that is present with God when separated from the body? . . . If souls separated from bodies did not retain their existence so as to be capable of glory and felicity, Christ would not have said to the thief, " To-day shalt thou be with me in paradise." (g) . . . Let us not hesitate, after the example of Christ, when we die, to commend our spirits to God; or, like Stephen, to resign them to the care of Christ, who is justly called the faithful " Shepherd and Bishop of souls." Over-curious inquiry respecting their interme-

---

(g) Luke xxiii. 43.

diate state is neither lawful nor useful. Many persons exceedingly perplex themselves by discussing what place they occupy, and whether they already enjoy the glory of heaven, or not. But it is folly and presumption to push our inquiries on unknown things beyond what God permits us to know. The Scripture declares that Christ is present with them, and receives them into paradise, where they enjoy consolation, and that the souls of the reprobate endure the torments which they have deserved; but it proceeds no further. Now, what teacher or doctor shall discover to us that which God has concealed? The question respecting place is equally senseless and futile; because we know that the soul has no dimensions like the body. . . . Let us be content within these limits which God prescribes to us — that the souls of pious men, after finishing their laborious warfare, depart into a state of blessed rest, where they wait with joy and pleasure for the fruition of the promised glory; and so, that all things remain in suspense till Christ appears as the Redeemer. . . .

Equally monstrous is the error of those who imagine that souls III. xxv. 7 will not resume the bodies which at present belong to them, but will be furnished with others altogether different. . . . Whatever we have in us now unworthy of heaven, will not hinder the resurrection. . . . Nor is there any point more clearly established in Scripture, than the resurrection of our present bodies. "This corruptible," says Paul, "must put on incorruption, and this mortal must put on immortality." (q) If new bodies were to be formed by God, what would become of this change of quality? . . . If we are to receive new bodies, where will be the conformity between the Head and members? Christ rose; was it by making himself a new body? No, but according to his prediction, "Destroy this temple, and in three days I will raise it up." (x) The mortal body which he before possessed, he again assumed. For it would have conducted but little to our benefit, if there had been a substitution of a new body, and an annihilation of that which had been offered as an atoning sacrifice. We must, therefore, maintain the connection stated by the apostle — that we shall rise, because Christ has risen; (y) for nothing is more improbable, than

---

(q) 1 Cor. xv. 54.   (x) John ii. 19.   (y) 1 Cor. xv. 12, &c.

that our body, in which "we bear about the dying of the Lord Jesus," (z) should be deprived of a resurrection similar to his. . . .

(3) A PROPER ATTITUDE NECESSARY

III. xxv. 8   It remains for me to touch a little on the manner of the resurrection. And I shall but just hint at it; because Paul, by calling it a mystery, exhorts us to sobriety, and forbids all licentiousness of subtle and extravagant speculation. In the first place, let it be remembered, as we have observed, that we shall rise again with the same bodies we have now, as to the substance, but that the quality will be different; just as the very body of Christ which had been offered as a sacrifice was raised again, but with such new and superior qualities, as though it had been altogether different. . . . There will be no necessity for any distance of time to intervene between death and the commencement of the next life; for " in a moment, in the twinkling of an eye, the trumpet shall sound, and the dead shall be raised incorruptible," (r) and the living transformed by a sudden change into the same glory. . . .

III. xxv. 10   Sobriety . . . is the more necessary for us on this subject, lest, forgetful of our slender capacity, we presumptuously soar to too high an elevation, and are overwhelmed with the blaze of celestial glory. We perceive, likewise, how we are actuated by an inordinate desire of knowing more than is right; which gives rise to a

III. xxv. 11   variety of questions, both frivolous and pernicious. . . . Men, thirsting after useless knowledge, inquire what will be the distance between the prophets and apostles, and between the apostles and martyrs; and how many degrees of difference there will be between those who have married and those who have lived and died in celibacy; in short, they leave not a corner of heaven unexplored. . . . The best and shortest rule for our conduct, is to content ourselves with " seeing through a glass darkly," till we shall " see face to face." (o) For very few persons are concerned about the way that leads to heaven, but all are anxious to know, before the time, what passes there. Men in general are slow, and reluctant to

---

(z) 2 Cor. iv. 10.   (r) 1 Cor. xv. 51, 52.   (o) 1 Cor. xiii. 12.

engage in the conflict and yet portray to themselves imaginary triumphs.

(4) THE DESTINY OF THE UNBELIEVER

Now, as no description can equal the severity of the Divine **III. xxv. 12** vengeance on the reprobate, their anguish and torment are figuratively represented to us under corporeal images; as, darkness, weeping, and gnashing of teeth, unextinguishable fire, a worm incessantly gnawing the heart. (*p*) For there can be no doubt but that, by such modes of expression, the Holy Spirit intended to confound all our faculties with horror. . . . As these representations should assist us in forming some conception of the wretched condition of the wicked, so they ought principally to fix our attention on the calamity of being alienated from the presence of God; and in addition to this, experiencing such hostility from the Divine majesty as to be unable to escape from its continual pursuit. . . . How great and severe . . . is the punishment, to endure the never ceasing effects of his wrath! On which subject there is a memorable passage in the ninetieth psalm; that though by his countenance he scatters all mortals, and turns them to destruction, yet he encourages his servants in proportion to their timidity in this world, to excite them, though under the burden of the cross, to press forward, till he shall be all in all.

(*p*) Matt. iii. 12; viii. 12; xxii. 13.   Mark ix. 43, 44.   Isaiah lxvi. 24.

Book IV

The Holy Catholic Church

CHAPTER XXI

The Nature and Function of the Church

❧

(1) NATURE: THE COMMUNION OF SAINTS

THAT by the faith of the gospel Christ becomes ours, and we become partakers of the salvation procured by him, and of eternal happiness, has been explained in the preceding Book. But as our ignorance and slothfulness, and, I may add, the vanity of our minds, require external aids, in order to the production of faith in our hearts, and its increase and progressive advance even to its completion, God has provided such aids in compassion to our infirmity; and that the preaching of the gospel might be maintained, he has deposited this treasure with the Church. He has appointed pastors and teachers, that his people might be taught by their lips; he has invested them with authority; in short, he has omitted nothing that could contribute to a holy unity of faith, and to the establishment of good order. (a) First of all, he has instituted Sacraments, which we know by experience to be means of the greatest utility for the nourishment and support of our faith, . . . prescribing a way in which we might approach him, notwithstanding our immense distance from him. Wherefore the order of

(a) Ephes. iv. 11—16.
151

instruction requires us now to treat of the Church and its government, orders, and power; secondly, of the Sacraments; and lastly,
of Civil Government. . . .

IV. i. 2　　That article of the Creed, in which we profess to believe THE
CHURCH, refers not only to the visible Church of which we are
now speaking, but likewise to all the elect of God, including the
dead as well as the living. The word BELIEVE is used, because it is
often impossible to discover any difference between the children of
God and the ungodly, between his peculiar flock and wild beasts.
The particle IN, interpolated by many, is not supported by any
probable reason. I confess that it is generally adopted at present,
and is not destitute of the suffrage of antiquity, being found in the
Nicene Creed, as it is transmitted to us in ecclesiastical history.
. . . We declare that we believe *in God* because our mind depends
upon him as true, and our confidence rests in him. But this would
not be applicable to the Church, any more than to " the remission
of sins," or the " resurrection of the body." Therefore, though I
am averse to contentions about words, yet I would rather adopt
a proper phraseology adapted to express the subject than affect
forms of expression by which the subject would be unnecessarily
involved in obscurity. . . .

The Church is called CATHOLIC, or universal; because there
could not be two or three churches, without Christ being divided,
which is impossible. But all the elect of God are so connected with
each other in Christ, that as they depend upon one head, so they
grow up together as into one body, compacted together like members of the same body; being made truly one, as living by one
faith, hope, and charity, through the same Divine Spirit, being
called not only to the same inheritance of eternal life, but also to a
participation of one God and Christ. . . .

IV. i. 3　　This article of the creed, however, relates in some measure to
the external Church, that every one of us may maintain a brotherly agreement with all the children of God, may pay due defer-
ence to the authority of the Church, and, in a word, may conduct
himself as one of the flock. Therefore we add THE COMMUNION OF
SAINTS — a clause which, though generally omitted by the ancients,
ought not to be neglected, because it excellently expresses the
character of the Church; as though it had been said that the saints

are united in the fellowship of Christ on this condition, that whatever benefits God confers upon them, they should mutually communicate to each other. . . . We believe the Church, in order to have a certain assurance that we are members of it. For thus our salvation rests on firm and solid foundations, so that it cannot fall into ruin, though the whole fabric of the world should be dissolved. First, it is founded on the election of God, and can be liable to no variation or failure, but with the subversion of his eternal providence. In the next place, it is united with the stability of Christ, who will no more suffer his faithful people to be severed from him, than his members to be torn in pieces. Besides, we are certain, as long as we continue in the bosom of the Church, that we shall remain in possession of the truth. Lastly, we understand these promises to belong to us: " In mount Zion shall be deliverance." (h) " God is in the midst of her; she shall not be moved." (i) Such is the effect of union with the Church, that it retains us in the fellowship of God. The very word *communion* likewise contains abundant consolation; for while it is certain that whatever the Lord confers upon his members and ours belong to us, our hope is confirmed by all the benefits which they enjoy. But in order to embrace the unity of the Church in this manner, it is unnecessary, as we have observed, to see the Church with our eyes, or feel it with our hands; on the contrary, from its being an object of faith, we are taught that it is no less to be considered as existing, when it escapes our observation, than if it were evident to our eyes. Nor is our faith the worse, because it acknowledges the Church which we do not fully comprehend; for we are not commanded here to distinguish the reprobate from the elect, which is not our province, but that of God alone; we are only required to be assured in our minds, that all those who, by the mercy of God the Father, through the efficacious influence of the Holy Spirit, have attained to the participation of Christ, are separated as the peculiar possession and portion of God; and that being numbered among them, we are partakers of such great grace.

But as our present design is to treat of the *visible* Church, we may learn even from the title of *mother,* how useful and even   IV. 1. 4

(h) Joel ii. 32. Obad. 17.   (i) Psalm xlvi. 5.

necessary it is for us to know her; since there is no other way of
entrance into life, unless we are conceived by her, born of her,
nourished at her breast, and continually preserved under her care
and government till we are divested of this mortal flesh, and " become like the angels." (k) . . . It is also to be remarked, that out
of her bosom there can be no hope of remission of sins, or any sal-

IV. 1. 5

vation. . . . But let us proceed to state what belongs to this subject. Paul writes, that Christ, " that he might fill all things, gave
some apostles, and some prophets, and some evangelists, and
some pastors and teachers; for the perfecting of the saints, for the
work of the ministry, for the edifying of the body of Christ: till
we all come in the unity of the faith, and of the knowledge of the
Son of God, unto a perfect man, unto the measure of the stature
of the fulness of Christ." (o) .We see that though God could easily
make his people perfect in a single moment, yet it was not his will
that they should grow to mature age, but under the education of
the Church. We see the means expressed; the preaching of the
heavenly doctrine is assigned to the pastors. We see that all are
placed under the same regulation, in order that they may submit
themselves with gentleness and docility of mind to be governed by
the pastors who are appointed for this purpose. . . . He not only
requires us to be attentive to reading, but has appointed teachers
for our assistance. This is attended with a twofold advantage. For
on the one hand, it is a good proof of our obedience when we listen
to his ministers, just as if he were addressing us himself; and on
the other, he has provided for our infirmity, by choosing to address us through the medium of human interpreters, that he may
sweetly allure us to him, rather than to drive us away from him by
his thunders. . . . Those who consider the authority of the doctrine as weakened by the meanness of the men who are called to
teach it, betray their ingratitude; because among so many excellent gifts with which God has adorned mankind, it is a peculiar
privilege, that he deigns to consecrate men's lips and tongues to
his service, that his voice may be heard in them. . . . Many are
urged by pride, or disdain, or envy, to persuade themselves that
they can profit sufficiently by reading and meditating in private,

---

(k) Matt. xxii. 30.   (o) Ephes. iv. 10—13.

and so to despise public assemblies, and consider preaching as unnecessary. But since they do all in their power to dissolve and break asunder the bond of unity, which ought to be preserved inviolable, not one of them escapes the just punishment of this impious breach, but they all involve themselves in pestilent errors and pernicious reveries. . . .

The word *Church* is frequently used in the Scriptures to designate the whole multitude, dispersed all over the world, who profess to worship one God and Jesus Christ, who are initiated into his faith by baptism, who testify their unity in true doctrine and charity by a participation of the sacred supper, who consent to the word of the Lord, and preserve the ministry which Christ has instituted for the purpose of preaching it. In this Church are included many hypocrites, who have nothing of Christ but the name and appearance; many persons ambitious, avaricious, envious, slanderous, and dissolute in their lives, who are tolerated for a time, either because they cannot be convicted by a legitimate process, or because discipline is not always maintained with sufficient vigour. As it is necessary, therefore, to believe that Church, which is invisible to us, and known to God alone, so this Church, which is visible to men, we are commanded to honour, and to maintain communion with it. . . . We ought to acknowledge as members of the Church all those who by a confession of faith, an exemplary life, and a participation of the sacraments, profess the same God and Christ with ourselves. But the knowledge of the body itself being more necessary to our salvation, he has distinguished it by more clear and certain characters.

Hence the visible Church rises conspicuous to our view. For wherever we find the word of God purely preached and heard, and the sacraments administered according to the institution of Christ, there, it is not to be doubted, is a Church of God; for his promise can never deceive — " where two or three are gathered together in my name, there am I in the midst of them." (*p*) But, that we may have a clear understanding of the whole of this subject, let us proceed by the following steps: That the universal Church is the whole multitude, collected from all nations, who,

_____

(*p*) Matt. xviii. 20.

though dispersed in countries widely distant from each other, nevertheless consent to the same truth of Divine doctrine, and are united by the bond of the same religion; that in this universal Church are comprehended particular churches, distributed according to human necessity in various towns and villages; and that each of these respectively is justly distinguished by the name and authority of a church; and that individuals, who, on a profession of piety, are enrolled among Churches of the same description, though they are really strangers to any particular Church, do nevertheless in some respect belong to it, till they are expelled from it by a public decision. There is some difference, however, in the mode of judging respecting private persons and churches. For it may happen, in the case of persons whom we think altogether unworthy of the society of the pious, that, on account of the common consent of the Church, by which they are tolerated in the body of Christ, we may be obliged to treat them as brethren, and to class them in the number of believers. In our private opinion we approve not of such persons as members of the Church, but we leave them the station they hold among the people of God, till it be taken away from them by legitimate authority. But respecting the congregation itself, we must form a different judgment. If they possess and honour the ministry of the word, and the administration of the sacraments, they are, without all doubt, entitled to be considered as a Church; because it is certain that the word and sacraments cannot be unattended with some good effects. In this manner, we preserve the unity of the universal Church, which diabolical spirits have always been endeavouring to destroy; and at the same time without interfering with the authority of those legitimate assemblies, which local convenience has distributed in different places. . . .

IV. i. 10   So highly does the Lord esteem the communion of his Church, that he considers every one as a traitor and apostate from religion, who perversely withdraws himself from any Christian society which preserves the true ministry of the word and sacraments. . . . A departure from the Church is a renunciation of God and

IV. i. 12   Christ. . . . When we affirm the pure ministry of the word, and pure order in the celebration of the sacraments, to be a sufficient pledge and earnest, that we may safely embrace the society in which both these are found, as a true Church, we carry the observation to this point, that such a society should never be rejected as long as it continues in those things, although in other respects it may be chargeable with many faults. It is possible, moreover, that some fault may insinuate itself into the preaching of the doctrine, or the administration of the sacraments, which ought not to alienate us from its communion. For all the articles of true doctrine are not of the same description. Some are so necessary to be known, that they ought to be universally received as fixed and indubitable principles, as the peculiar maxims of religion; such as, that there is one God; that Christ is God and the Son of God; that our salvation depends on the mercy of God; and the like. There are others, which are controverted among the churches, yet without destroying the unity of the faith. . . . Diversity of opinion respecting . . . non-essential points ought not to be a cause of discord among Christians. . . . It is of importance, indeed, that we should agree in everything; but as there is no person who is not enveloped with some cloud of ignorance, either we must allow of no church at all, or we must forgive mistakes in those things, of which persons may be ignorant, without violating the essence of religion, or incurring the loss of salvation. Here I would not be understood to plead for any errors, even the smallest, or to recommend their being encouraged by connivance or flattery. But I maintain, that we ought not, on account of every trivial difference of sentiment, to abandon the Church, which retains the saving and pure doctrine that insures the preservation of piety, and supports the use of the sacraments instituted by our Lord. . . . Every member of the Church is required to exert himself for the general edification, according to the measure of his grace, provided he do it decently and in order; that is to say, that we should neither forsake the communion of the Church, nor, by continuing in it, disturb its peace and well regulated discipline. . . .

For since it is the will of God that the communion of his Church ᴵⱽ. ᵢ. 16 should be maintained in this external society, those who, from an aversion of wicked men, destroy the token of that society, enter on a course in which they are in great danger of falling from the communion of saints. Let them consider, in the first place, that in a great multitude there are many who escape their observation, who, nevertheless, are truly holy and innocent in the sight of God. Secondly, let them consider, that of those who appear subject to moral maladies, there are many who by no means please or flatter themselves in their vices, but are oftentimes aroused, with a serious fear of God, to aspire to greater integrity. Thirdly, let them consider that judgment ought not to be pronounced upon a man from a single act, since the holiest persons have sometimes most grievous falls. Fourthly, let them consider, that the ministry of the word, and the participation of the sacraments, have too much influence in preserving the unity of the Church, to admit of its being destroyed by the guilt of a few impious men. Lastly, let them consider, that in forming an estimate of the Church, the judgment of God is of more weight than that of man. . . .

IV. i. 17   It is necessary to examine the holiness in which [the Church] . . . excels. . . . The Church . . . is so far holy, that it is daily improving, but has not yet arrived at perfection; that it is daily advancing, but has not yet reached the mark of holiness; as in another part of this work will be more fully explained. The predictions of the prophets, therefore, that " Jerusalem shall be holy, and there shall no strangers pass through her any more," and that the way of God shall be a " way of holiness," over which " the unclean shall not pass," (e) are not to be understood as if there were no blemish remaining in any of the members of the Church; but because they aspire with all their souls towards perfect holiness and purity, the goodness of God attributes to them that sanctity to which they have not yet fully attained. . . .

IV. i. 19   Let these two points, then, be considered as decided; first, that he who voluntarily deserts the external communion of the Church where the word of God is preached, and the sacraments are administered, is without any excuse; secondly, that the faults either of few persons or of many, form no obstacles to a due profession of our faith in the use of the ceremonies instituted by God; because the pious conscience is not wounded by the unworthiness of any other individual, whether he be a pastor or a private person; nor are the mysteries less pure and salutary to a holy and upright man, because they are received at the same time by the impure. . . .

(e) Joel iii. 17.   Isaiah xxxv. 8.

(2) FUNCTION: THE FORGIVENESS OF SINS

In the Creed, *the communion of saints* is immediately followed IV. i. 20
by *the forgiveness of sins,* which can only be obtained by the citizens and members of the Church, as we read in the prophet. (*i*)
. . . Our first entrance, therefore, into the Church and kingdom
of God, is the remission of sins, without which we have no covenant
or union with God. . . . Nor does God only once receive and IV. i. 21
adopt us into his Church by the remission of sins; he likewise preserves and keeps us in it by the same mercy. For to what purpose
would it be, if we obtained a pardon which would afterwards be of
no use? And that the mercy of the Lord would be vain and delu-
sive, if it were only granted for once, all pious persons can testify
to themselves; for every one of them is all his life-time conscious
of many infirmities, which need the Divine mercy. And surely it is
not without reason, that God particularly promises this grace to
the members of his family, and commands the same message of
reconciliation to be daily addressed to them. As we carry about
with us the relics of sin, therefore, as long as we live, we shall
scarcely continue in the Church for a single moment, unless we are
sustained by the constant grace of the Lord in forgiving our sins.
But the Lord has called his people to eternal salvation; they
ought, therefore, to believe that his grace is always ready to pardon
their sins. Wherefore it ought to be held as a certain conclusion,
that from the Divine liberality, by the intervention of the merit of
Christ, through the sanctification of the Spirit, pardon of sins has
been, and is daily, bestowed upon us, who have been admitted and
ingrafted into the body of the Church. . . .

Here are three things, therefore, worthy of our observation. IV. i. 22
First, that whatever holiness may distinguish the children of God,
yet such is their condition as long as they inhabit a mortal body,
that they cannot stand before God without remission of sins. Secondly, that this benefit belongs to the Church; so that we cannot
enjoy it unless we continue in its communion. Thirdly, that it is
dispensed to us by the ministers and pastors of the Church, either
in the preaching of the gospel, or in the administration of the

---

(*i*) Isaiah xxxiii. 24.

sacraments; and that this is the principal exercise of the power of the keys, which the Lord has conferred on the society of believers. (*m*) . . . Let every one of us, therefore, consider it as his duty, not to seek remission of sins any where but where the Lord has placed it. . . .

(*m*) Matt. xvi. 19; xviii. 18.

CHAPTER XXII

The Government of the Church

❧

(1) ORDAINED BY GOD

WE MUST now treat of the order which it has been the Lord's will to appoint for the government of his Church. For although he alone ought to rule and reign in the Church, and to have all preëminence in it, and this government ought to be exercised and administered solely by his word, — yet, as he dwells not among us by a visible presence, so as to make an audible declaration of his will to us, we have stated, that for this purpose he uses the ministry of men whom he employs as his delegates, not to transfer his right and honour to them, but only that he may himself do his work by their lips; just as an artificer makes use of an instrument in the performance of his work. . . . In the first place, by this method he declares his kindness towards us, since he chooses from among men those who are to be his ambassadors to the world, to be the interpreters of his secret will, and even to act as his personal representatives. And thus he affords an actual proof, that when he so frequently calls us his temples, it is not an unmeaning appellation, since he gives answers to men, even from the mouths of men, as from a sanctuary. In the second place, this is a most excellent and beneficial method to train us to humility, since he accustoms us to obey his word, though it is preached to us by men like ourselves, and sometimes even of inferior rank. If he were himself to speak from heaven, there would be no wonder if his sacred oracles were instantly received with reverence, by the ears and hearts of all mankind. For who would not be awed by his present power? who would not fall prostrate at the first view of infinite Majesty? who would not be confounded by that over-powering splendour? But when a contemptible mortal, who had just emerged from the dust, addresses us in the name of God, we give the best evidence of our piety and reverence towards God himself, if we readily submit to be instructed by his minister, who possesses no personal superiority to ourselves. For this reason, also, he has deposited the treasure of his heavenly wisdom in frail and earthen vessels, (a) in order to afford a better proof of the estimation in which we hold it. Besides, nothing was more adapted to promote brotherly love, than a mutual connection of men by this bond, while one is constituted the pastor to teach all the rest, and they who are commanded to be disciples, receive one common doctrine from the same mouth. For if each person were sufficient for himself, and had no need of the assistance of another, such is the pride of human nature, every one would despise others, and would also be despised by them. The Lord, therefore, has connected his Church together, by that which he foresaw would be the strongest bond for the preservation of their union, when he committed the doctrine of eternal life and salvation to men, that by their hands it might be communicated to others. . . .

IV. iii. 2   Whoever, therefore, either aims to abolish or undervalue this order, of which we are treating, and this species of government, attempts to disorganize the Church, or rather to subvert and destroy it altogether. For neither the light and heat of the sun, nor any meat and drink, are so necessary to the nourishment and sustenance of the present life, as the apostolical and pastoral office is to the preservation of the Church in the world. . . .

(a) 2 Cor. iv. 7.

(2) THE OFFICERS OF THE CHURCH AND
THEIR DUTIES

Those who preside over the government of the Church, ac-   IV. iii. 4
cording to the institution of Christ, are named by Paul, first,
" apostles; " secondly, " prophets; " thirdly, " evangelists; "
fourthly, " pastors; " lastly, " teachers." (h) Of these, only the
two last sustain an ordinary office in the Church: the others were
such as the Lord raised up at the commencement of his kingdom,
and such as he still raises up on particular occasions, when required by the necessity of the times. The nature of the apostolic
office is manifest from this command: " Go preach the gospel to
every creature." (i) No certain limits are prescribed, but the whole
world is assigned to them, to be reduced to obedience to Christ;
that by disseminating the gospel wherever they could, they might
erect his kingdom in all nations. . . . The " apostles," therefore,
were missionaries, who were to reduce the world from their revolt
to true obedience to God, and to establish his kingdom universally
by the preaching of the gospel. Or, if you please, they were the
first architects of the Church, appointed to lay its foundations all
over the world. Paul gives the appellation of " prophets," not to
all interpreters of the Divine will, but only to those who were
honoured with some special revelation. Of these, either there are
none in our day, or they are less conspicuous. By " evangelists,"
I understand those who were inferior to the apostles in dignity,
but next to them in office, and who performed similar functions.
Such were Luke, Timothy, Titus, and others of that description;
and perhaps also the seventy disciples, whom Christ ordained to
occupy the second station from the apostles. (k) According to this
interpretation, which appears to me perfectly consistent with the
language and meaning of the apostle, those three offices were not
instituted to be of perpetual continuance in the Church, but only
for that age when Churches were to be raised where none had
existed before, or were at least to be conducted from Moses to
Christ. Though I do not deny, that, even since that period, God

---

(h) Eph. iv. 11.   (i) Mark xvi. 15.   (k) Luke x. 1.

has sometimes raised up apostles or evangelists in their stead, as he has done in our own time. For there was a necessity for such persons to recover the Church from the defection of Antichrist. Nevertheless, I call this an extraordinary office, because it has no place in well-constituted Churches. Next follow "pastors" and "teachers," who are always indispensable to the Church. The difference between them I apprehend to be this — that teachers have no official concern with the discipline, or the administration of the sacraments, or with admonitions and exhortations, but only with the interpretation of the Scripture, that pure and sound doctrine may be retained among believers; whereas the pastoral office includes all these things.

IV. iii. 5　We have now ascertained what offices were appointed to continue for a time in the government of the Church, and what were instituted to be of perpetual duration. If we connect the evangelists with the apostles, as sustaining the same office, we shall then have two offices of each description, corresponding to each other. For our pastors bear the same resemblance to the apostles, as our teachers do to the ancient prophets. . . .

IV. iii. 6　Our Lord, when he sent forth his apostles, commissioned them, as we have just remarked, to preach the gospel, and to baptize all believers for the remission of sins. (m) He had already commanded them to distribute the sacred symbols of his body and blood according to his own example. (n) Behold the sacred, inviolable, and perpetual law imposed upon those who call themselves successors of the apostles; it commands them to preach the gospel, and to administer the sacraments. Hence we conclude, that those who neglect both these duties have no just pretensions to the character of apostles. But what shall we say of pastors? Paul speaks not only of himself, but of all who bear that office, when he says, "Let a man so account of us, as of the ministers of Christ, and stewards of the mysteries of God." (o) Again: "A bishop must hold fast the faithful word as he hath been taught, that he may be able, by sound doctrine, both to exhort and to convince the gainsayers." (p) From these and similar passages, which frequently occur, we may infer that the preaching of the

---

(m) Matt. xxviii. 19.　　　　(n) Luke xxii. 19.
(o) 1 Cor. iv. 1.　　　　　　　(p) Titus i. 7, 9.

gospel, and the administration of the sacraments, constitute the two principal parts of the pastoral office. Now, the business of teaching is not confined to public discourses, but extends also to private admonitions. Thus Paul calls upon the Ephesians to witness the truth of his declaration, " I have kept back nothing that was profitable unto you, but have showed you, and have taught you publicly, and from house to house, testifying both to the Jews, and also to the Greeks, repentance toward God, and faith toward our Lord Jesus Christ." And a little after: " I ceased not to warn every one, night and day, with tears." (q) . . .

In calling those who preside over Churches by the appellations **IV. iii. 8** of bishops, elders, pastors, and ministers, without any distinction, I have followed the usage of the Scripture, which applies all these terms to express the same meaning. . . . " Governors " (c) I apprehend to have been persons of advanced years, selected from the people, to unite with the bishops in giving admonitions and exercising discipline. . . . From the beginning, every Church has had its senate or council, composed of pious, grave, and holy men, who were invested with that jurisdiction in the correction of vices. . . . The care of the poor was committed to the " deacons." The **IV. iii. 9** Epistle to the Romans, however, mentions two functions of this kind. " He that giveth," says the apostle, " let him do it with simplicity: he that showeth mercy, with cheerfulness." (e) Now, as it is certain that he there speaks of the public offices of the Church, it follows that there were two distinct orders of deacons. Unless my judgment deceive me, the former clause refers to the deacons who administered the alms; and the other to those who devoted themselves to the care of poor and sick persons; such as the widows mentioned by Paul to Timothy. (f) . . .

(3) THE MINISTRY: ORDINATION AND INDUCTION

Now, as " all things " in the Church are required to " be done **IV. iii. 10** decently and in order," (h) there is nothing in which this ought to be more diligently observed, than the constitution of its government; because there would be more danger from disorder in

---

(q) Acts xx. 20, 21, 31.   (c) 1 Cor. xii. 28.   (e) Rom. xii. 8.
    (f) 1 Tim. v. 9, 10.   (h) 1 Cor. xiv. 40.

this case than in any other. . . . In order, therefore, that any one may be accounted a true minister of the Church, it is necessary, in the first place, that he be regularly called to it, and, in the second place, that he answer his call; that is, by undertaking and executing the office assigned to him. . . . Let us . . . confine ourselves to the call. . . .

IV. iii. 11   The discussion of this subject includes four branches: what are the qualifications of ministers; in what manner they are to be chosen; by whom they ought to be appointed; and with what rite or ceremony they are to be introduced into their office. I speak of the external and solemn call, which belongs to the public order of the Church; passing over that secret call, of which every minister is conscious to himself before God, but which is not known to the Church. . . .

IV. iii. 12   The qualifications of those who ought to be chosen bishops, are stated at large by Paul in two passages. (k) The sum of all he says is, that none are to be chosen but men of sound doctrine and a holy life, not chargeable with any fault that may destroy their authority, or disgrace their ministry. . . .

The question relating to the *manner* in which they are to be chosen, I refer not to the form of election, but to the religious awe which ought to be observed in it. Hence the fasting and prayer, which Luke states to have been practised by the faithful at the ordination of elders. (n) For knowing themselves to be engaged in a business of the highest importance, they dared not attempt any thing but with the greatest reverence and solicitude. And above all things, they were earnest in prayers and supplications to God for the spirit of wisdom and discretion.

IV. iii. 13   The third inquiry we proposed was, by whom ministers are to be chosen. Now, for this no certain rule can be gathered from the appointment of the apostles, which was a case somewhat different

IV. iii. 14   from the common call of other ministers. . . . But that the election and appointment of bishops by men is necessary to constitute a legitimate call to the office, no sober person will deny, while there

IV. iii. 15   are so many testimonies of Scripture to establish it. . . . Here it is inquired, whether a minister ought to be chosen by the whole

---

(k) 1 Tim. iii. 1, &c. Titus i. 7, &c.   (n) Acts xiv. 23.

Church, or only by the other ministers and the elders who preside over the discipline, or whether he may be appointed by the authority of an individual. . . . It is a legitimate ministry according to the word of God, when those who appear suitable persons are appointed with the consent and approbation of the people; but . . . other pastors ought to preside over the election, to guard the multitude from falling into any improprieties, through inconstancy, intrigue, or confusion.

There remains the Form of ordination, which is the last point IV. iii. 16 that we have mentioned relative to the call of ministers. Now, it appears that when the apostles introduced any one into the ministry, they used no other ceremony than imposition of hands. . . . Though there is no express precept for the imposition of hands, yet since we find it to have been constantly used by the apostles, such a punctual observance of it by them ought to have the force of a precept with us. And certainly this ceremony is highly useful both to recommend to the people the dignity of the ministry, and to admonish the person ordained that he is no longer his own master, but devoted to the service of God and the Church. . . .

CHAPTER XXIII

The Authority of the Church

✣

(1) DOCTRINE AND THE WORD OF GOD

THE next subject is the power of the Church, which is to be considered as residing, partly in the respective bishops, partly in councils, and those either provincial or general. I speak only of the spiritual power which belongs to the Church. Now, it consists either in doctrine, in legislation, or jurisdiction. The subject of doctrine contains two parts — the authority to establish doctrines, and the explication of them. . . . Now, the only way to edify the Church is, for the ministers themselves to study to preserve to Jesus Christ his rightful authority, which can no longer be secure than while he is left in possession of what he has received from the Father, that is, to be the sole Master in the Church. (*i*) For of him alone, and of no other, is it said, "Hear ye him." (*k*) The power of the Church, therefore, is not to be depreciated, yet it must be circumscribed by certain limits, that it may not be extended in every direction, according to the caprice of men. . . .

Here, therefore, it is necessary to remember, that whatever authority and dignity is attributed by the Holy Spirit, in the Scripture, either to the priests and prophets under the law, or to the apostles and their successors, it is all given, not in a strict

---

(*i*) Matt. xxiii. 8.   (*k*) Matt. xvii. 5.

sense to the persons themselves, but to the ministry over which they were appointed, or, to speak more correctly, to the word, the ministration of which was committed to them. For if we examine them all in succession, we shall not find that they were invested with any authority to teach or to answer inquiries, but in the name and word of the Lord. For when they were called to their office, it was at the same time enjoined that they should bring forward nothing of themselves, but should speak from the mouth of the Lord. Nor did he send them forth in public to address the people, before he had instructed them what they should say, that they might speak nothing beside his word. . . .

But whereas it has been a principle received in the Church IV. viii. 5 from the beginning, and ought to be admitted in the present day, that the servants of God should teach nothing which they have not learned from him, yet they have had different modes of receiving instruction from him, according to the variety of different periods; and the present mode differs from those which have preceded it. In the first place, if the assertion of Christ be true, that " no man knoweth the Father except the Son, and he to whomsoever the Son will reveal him," (a) it must always have been necessary for those who would arrive at the knowledge of God, to be directed by that eternal wisdom. For how could they have comprehended the mysteries of God, or how could they have declared them, except by the teaching of him, to whom alone the secrets of the Father are intimately known? . . . But this wisdom has not always manifested itself in the same way. With the patriarchs God employed secret revelations; for the confirmation of which, however, he at the same time added such signs that they could not entertain the least doubt that it was God who spake to them. What the patriarchs had received, they transmitted from hand to hand to their posterity; for the Lord had committed it to them on the express condition that they should so propagate it. Succeeding generations, from the testimony of God in their hearts, knew that what they heard was from heaven, and not from the earth.

But when it pleased God to raise up a more visible form of IV. viii. 6 a church, it was his will that his word should be committed to

---

(a) Matt. xi. 27.

writing, in order that the priests might derive from it whatever they would communicate to the people, and that all the doctrine which should be delivered might be examined by that rule. Therefore, after the promulgation of the law, when the priests were commanded to teach " out of the mouth of the Lord," the meaning is, that they should teach nothing extraneous, or different from that system of doctrine which the Lord had comprised in the law; it was not lawful for them to add to it or to diminish from it. Afterwards followed the prophets, by whom God published new oracles, which were to be added to the law; yet they were not so new but that they proceeded from the law, and bore a relation to it. For in regard to doctrine, the prophets were merely interpreters of the law, and added nothing to it except prophecies of things to come. Except these, they brought forward nothing but pure explication of the law. But because it pleased God that there should be a more evident and copious doctrine, for the better satisfaction of weak consciences, he directed the prophecies also to be committed to writing, and to be accounted a part of his word. To these likewise were added the histories, which were the productions of the prophets, but composed under the dictation of the Holy Spirit. I class the Psalms with the prophecies, because what we attribute to the prophecies is common to the Psalms. That whole body of Scripture, therefore, consisting of the Law, the Prophets, the Psalms, and the Histories, was the word of God to the ancient Church; and to this standard the priests and teachers, even to the coming of Christ, were bound to conform their doctrine; nor was it lawful for them to deviate either to the right hand or to the left, because their office was wholly confined within these limits, that they should answer the people from the mouth of God. . . .

IV. viii. 7   But when, at length, the Wisdom of God was manifested in the flesh, it openly declared to us all that the human mind is capable of comprehending, or ought to think, concerning the heavenly Father. Now, therefore, since Christ, the Sun of Righteousness, has shone upon us, we enjoy the full splendour of Divine truth, resembling the brightness of noonday, whereas the light enjoyed before was a kind of twilight. For certainly the apostle intended to state no unimportant fact when he said, that " God, who, at

sundry times, and in divers manners, spake in time past unto the
fathers by the prophets, hath in these last days spoken unto us
by his Son; " (c) for he here suggests, and even plainly declares, that God will not in future, as in ages past, speak from
time to time by one and another, that he will not add prophecies
to prophecies, or revelations to revelations, but that he has com-
pleted all the branches of instruction in his Son, so that this is
the last and eternal testimony that we shall have from him; for
which reason this whole period of the New Testament, from the
appearance of Christ to us in the first promulgation of his gospel,
even to the day of judgment, is designated as " the last time,"
" the last times," " the last days; " in order that, being content
with the perfection of the doctrine of Christ, we may learn neither
to invent any thing new or beyond it ourselves, nor to receive
any such thing from the invention of others. It is not without
cause, therefore, that the Father has given us his Son by a peculiar
privilege, and appointed him to be our teacher, commanding
attention to be paid to him, and not to any mere man. He has
recommended his tuition to us in few words, when he says, " Hear
ye him; " (d) but there is more weight and energy in them than
is commonly imagined; for they call us away from all the instructions of men, and place us before him alone; they command us to learn from him alone all the doctrine of salvation, to
depend upon him, to adhere to him, in short, as the words express,
to listen solely to his voice. And, indeed, what ought now to be
either expected or desired from man, when the Word of Life
himself has familiarly presented himself before us? It is rather
necessary that the mouths of all men should be shut, since he has
once spoken, in whom it has pleased the heavenly Father that all
the treasures of wisdom and knowledge should be hidden, (e)
and has spoken in a manner becoming the wisdom of God, in
which there is no imperfection, and the Messiah, who was expected to reveal all things; (f) that is, has spoken in such a
manner as to leave nothing to be said by others after him.

Let us lay down this, then, as an undoubted axiom, that nothing   IV. viii. 8

(c) Heb. i. 1, 2.   (d) Matt. xvii. 5.
(e) Col. i. 19; ii. 3.   (f) John iv. 25.

ought to be admitted in the Church as the word of God, but what is contained first in the law and the prophets, and secondly in the writings of the apostles, and that there is no other method of teaching aright in the Church than according to the direction and standard of that word. . . . This is the extent of the power with which the pastors of the Church, by whatever name they may be distinguished, ought to be invested; — that by the word of God they may venture to do all things with confidence; may constrain all the strength, glory, wisdom, and pride of the world to obey and submit to his majesty; supported by his power, may govern all mankind, from the highest to the lowest; may build up the house of Christ, and subvert the house of Satan; may feed the sheep, and drive away the wolves; may instruct and exhort the docile; may reprove, rebuke, and restrain the rebellious and obstinate; may bind and loose; may discharge their lightnings and thunders, if necessary; but all in the word of God. Between the apostles and their successors, however, there is, as I have stated, this differ-ence — that the apostles were the certain and authentic amanu-enses of the Holy Spirit, and therefore their writings are to be received as the oracles of God; but succeeding ministers have no other office than to teach what is revealed and recorded in the sacred Scriptures. We conclude, then, that it is not now left to faithful ministers to frame any new doctrine, but that it behoves them simply to adhere to the doctrine to which God has made all subject, without any exception. In making this observation, my design is to show, not only what is lawful to individuals, but also to the universal Church. . . .

IV. viii. 9

(2) THE LAW OF GOD AND THE LAW OF MEN

IV. x. 1

We now proceed to the second branch of the power of the Church, . . . legislation. . . . This power is now to be examined — whether the Church has authority to make laws which shall bind the consciences of men. This question has nothing to do with political order; the only objects of our present attention are, that God may be rightly worshipped according to the rule he has prescribed, and that our spiritual liberty which relates to God may be preserved entire. . . . I only contend for this one point, that no necessity ought to be imposed upon consciences in things in which they have been set at liberty by Christ; and without this liberty, as I have before observed, they can have no peace with God. They must acknowledge Christ their Deliverer as their only King, and must be governed by one law of liberty, even the sacred word of the gospel, if they wish to retain the grace which they have once obtained in Christ; they must submit to no slavery; they must be fettered by no bonds. . . .

The generality of men . . . are embarrassed with this ques- IV. x. 3
tion, for want of distinguishing with sufficient exactness between the outward judgment of men and the court of conscience. The difficulty is increased by the injunction of Paul, that the magistrate is to be obeyed, " not only for wrath, but also for conscience' sake; " (h) whence it follows, that consciences are bound by political laws. If this were the case, all that we . . . are about to say . . . on the subject of spiritual government, would fall to the ground. To solve this difficulty, it is first of all necessary to understand what is conscience. The definition may be derived from the etymology of the word. *Science,* or *knowledge,* is the apprehension which men have of things in their mind and understanding. So, when they have an apprehension of the judgment of God, as a witness that suffers them not to conceal their sins, but forces them as criminals before the tribunal of the judge, this apprehension is called *conscience.* For it is something between God and man, which permits not a man to suppress what he knows within himself, but pursues him till it brings him to a sense of his guilt. This is what Paul means, when he speaks of men's " conscience also bearing witness, and their thoughts the mean while accusing, or else excusing, one another " (i) before God. A simple knowledge might remain in man, as it were, in a state of concealment. Therefore this sentiment, which places men before the tribunal of God, is like a keeper appointed over man to watch and observe all his secrets, that nothing may remain buried in darkness. Hence that old proverb, that conscience is equal to a thousand witnesses. . . . Therefore, as works have respect IV. x. 4

(h) Rom. xiii. 5.   (i) Rom. ii. 15.

to man, so the conscience is referred to God. A good conscience is no other than an internal purity of heart. . . . Hence it is, that a law is said to bind the conscience, which simply binds a man without any observation or consideration of other men. For example, God not only commands the heart to be preserved chaste and pure from every libidinous desire, but prohibits all obscenity of language and external lasciviousness. My conscience is bound to observe this law, even though not another man existed in the world. The person, therefore, who commits any breach of chastity, not only sins by setting a bad example to his brethren, but brings his conscience into a state of guilt before God. The case of things, in themselves indifferent, stands not on the same ground; for we ought to abstain from whatever is likely to give offence, but with a free conscience. . . .

V. x. 5   Let us now return to human laws. If they are designed to introduce any scruple into our minds, as though the observance of them were essentially necessary, we assert, that they are unreasonable impositions on the conscience. For our consciences have to do, not with men, but with God alone. . . . But we have not yet solved the difficulty which arises from the language of Paul. For if princes are to be obeyed, " not only for wrath, but also for conscience' sake," (q) it seems to follow, that the laws of princes have dominion over the conscience. If this be true, the same must be affirmed of the laws of the Church. I reply, In the first place, it is necessary to distinguish between the *genus* and the *species*. For the conscience is not affected by every particular law; yet we are bound by the general command of God, which establishes the authority of magistrates. And this is the hinge upon which Paul's argument turns, that magistrates are to be honoured because they are " ordained of God." (r) At the same time he is far from insinuating that the laws enacted by them have any thing to do with the internal government of the soul; for he every where extols the service of God and the spiritual rule of a holy life, above all the statutes and decrees of men. A second consideration worthy of notice, which is a consequence of the first, is, that human laws, — I mean such as are good and just, whether enacted by magis-

(q) Rom. xiii. 5   (r) Rom. xiii. 1.

trates or by the Church, — though they are necessary to be observed, are not on this account binding on the conscience; because all the necessity of observing them has reference to the general object of laws, but does not consist in the particular things which are commanded. There is an immense distance between laws of this description, and those which prescribe any new form for the worship of God, and impose a necessity in things that were left free and indifferent. . . .

Every thing pertaining to the perfect rule of a holy life, the Lord has comprehended in his law, so that there remains nothing for men to add to that summary. And he has done this, first, that, since all rectitude of life consists in the conformity of all our actions to his will, as their standard, we might consider him as the sole Master and Director of our conduct; and secondly, to show that he requires of us nothing more than obedience. . . . IV. x. 7

If . . . any one wish to have a simple statement, what are the human traditions of all ages, which ought to be rejected and reprobated by the Church and all pious persons . . . — they are all laws made by men without the word of God, for the purpose, either of prescribing any method for the worship of God, or of laying the conscience under a religious obligation, as if they enjoined things necessary to salvation. If either or both of these be accompanied with other faults, such as, that the ceremonies, by their multitude, obscure the simplicity of the gospel; that they tend to no edification, but are useless and ridiculous occupations rather than real exercises of piety; that they are employed for the sordid purposes of dishonest gain; that they are too difficult to be observed; that they are polluted with impious superstitions; — these things will further assist us in discovering the vast evil which they contain. . . . IV. x. 16

But, as many ignorant persons, when they hear that the consciences of men ought not to be bound by human traditions, and that it is in vain to worship God by such services immediately conclude the same rule to be applicable to all the laws which regulate the order of the Church, we must also refute their error. It is easy, indeed, to be deceived in this point, because it does not immediately appear, at the first glance, what a difference there is between the one and the other; but I will place the whole subject IV. x. 27

in such a clear light, in a few words, that no one may be misled by the resemblance. In the first place, let us consider that if, in every society of men, we see the necessity of some polity in order to preserve the common peace, and to maintain concord; if in the transaction of business there is always some order, which the interest of public virtue, and even of humanity itself, forbids to be rejected, the same ought particularly to be observed in Churches, which are best supported by a well-ordered regulation of all their affairs and which without concord are no Churches at all. Wherefore, if we would make a proper provision for the safety of the Church, we ought to pay the strictest attention to the injunction of Paul, that " all things be done decently and in order." (*i*) But as there is such great diversity in the manners of men, so great a variety in their minds, and so much contrariety in their judgments and inclinations, no polity will be sufficiently steady unless it be established by certain laws; nor can any order be preserved without some settled form. The laws, therefore, which promote this end, we are so far from condemning, that, we contend, their abolition would be followed by a disruption of the bands of union, and the total disorganization and dispersion of the Churches. For it is impossible to attain what Paul requires, that " all things be done decently and in order," unless order and decorum be supported by additional regulations. But in regard to such regulations, care must always be taken, that they be not considered necessary to salvation, and so imposing a religious obligation on the conscience, or applied to the worship of God, and so represented as essential to piety.

We have an excellent and most certain mark, therefore, which distinguishes those impious constitutions, by which it has been stated that true religion is obscured and men's consciences subverted, and the legitimate regulations of the Church, which are always directed to one of these two ends, or to both together; that, in the holy assembly of believers, all things may be conducted with suitable decorum and dignity, that the community may be kept in order by the firm bonds of courtesy and moderation. For when it is once understood that a law is made for the

---

(*i*) 1 Cor. xiv. 40.

sake of public order, this removes the superstition embraced by them who place the worship of God in human inventions. More-over, when it is known that it only refers to matters of common practice, this overturns all that false notion of obligation and necessity, which filled men's consciences with great terror, when traditions were thought necessary to salvation. For here nothing is required but the maintenance of charity among us by the com-mon intercourse of friendly offices. But it is proper to describe more fully what is comprehended under the decorum and the order which Paul recommends. The end of *decorum* is, partly, that while ceremonies are employed to conciliate veneration to sacred things, we may be excited to piety by such aids; partly that the modesty and gravity, which ought to be discovered in all virtuous actions, may be most of all conspicuous in the Church. In *order*, the first point is, that those who preside should be ac-quainted with the rule and law of good government, and that the people who are governed should be accustomed to an obedience to God and to just discipline; the second is, that when the Church is in a well regulated state, care should be taken to preserve its peace and tranquillity. . . .

I approve of no human constitutions, except such as are founded IV. x. 30 on the authority of God, and deduced from the Scripture, so that they may be considered as altogether Divine. Let us take, as an example, the kneeling practised during solemn prayers. The question is, whether it be a human tradition, which every one is at liberty to reject or neglect. I answer that it is at once both human and Divine. It is of God, as it forms a branch of that decorum which is recommended to our attention and observance by the apostle; it is of men, as it particularly designates that which had in general been rather hinted than clearly expressed. From this single example, it is easy to judge what opinion ought to be entertained of all the rest. Because the Lord, in his holy oracles, has faithfully comprehended and plainly declared to us the whole nature of true righteousness, and all the parts of Divine worship, with whatever is necessary to salvation, — in these things he is to be regarded as our only Master. Because, in external discipline and ceremonies, he has not been pleased to give us minute directions what we ought to do in every particular case,

foreseeing that this would depend on the different circumstances
of different periods, and knowing that one form would not be
adapted to all ages, — here we must have recourse to the general
rules which he has given, that to them may be conformed all the
regulations which shall be necessary to the decorum and order
of the Church. Lastly, as he has delivered no express injunctions
on this subject, because these things are not necessary to salvation, and ought to be applied to the edification of the Church,
with a variety suitable to the manners of each age and nation,
therefore, as the benefit of the Church shall require, it will be
right to change and abolish former regulations, and to institute
new ones. I grant, indeed, that we ought not to resort to innovation
rashly or frequently, or for trivial causes. But charity will best
decide what will injure or edify, and if we submit to the dictates
of charity, all will be well. . . .

(3) THE SPIRITUAL JURISDICTION OF THE CHURCH

IV. xi. 1   We come now to the third branch of the power of the Church,
and that which is the principal one in a well regulated state, which
we have said consists in jurisdiction. The whole jurisdiction of the
Church relates to the discipline of manners. . . . For as no city
or town can exist without a magistracy and civil polity, so the
Church of God . . . stands in need of a certain spiritual polity;
which, however, is entirely distinct from civil polity, and is so
far from obstructing or weakening it, that, on the contrary, it
highly conduces to its assistance and advancement. This power
of jurisdiction, therefore, will, in short, be no other than an order
instituted for the preservation of the spiritual polity. For this
end, there were from the beginning judiciaries appointed in the
Churches, to take cognizance of manners, to pass censures on vices,
and to preside over the use of the keys in excommunication. . . .

IV. xi. 3   The Church has no power of the sword to punish or to coerce,
no authority to compel, no prisons, fines, or other punishments,
like those inflicted by the civil magistrate. Besides, the object of
this power is, not that he who has transgressed may be punished
against his will but that he may profess his repentance by a voluntary submission to chastisement. The difference therefore is very

great; because the Church does not assume to itself what belongs to the magistrate, nor can the magistrate execute that which is executed by the Church. . . . But as it is the duty of the magistrate, by punishment and corporeal coercion, to purge the Church from offences, so it behoves the minister of the word, on his part, to relieve the magistrate by preventing the multiplication of offenders. Their respective operations ought to be so connected as to be an assistance, and not an obstruction to each other. . . . The jurisdiction of the Church . . . ought to . . . secure . . .   IV. xi. 5 the prevention of offences, or the abolition of any that may have arisen. In the use of it, two things require to be considered; first, that this spiritual power be entirely separated from the power of the sword; secondly, that it be administered. not at the pleasure of one man, but by a legitimate assembly. . . .

(4) THE MAINTENANCE OF DISCIPLINE

The discipline of the Church . . . depends chiefly on the power   IV. xii. 1 of the keys, and the spiritual jurisdiction. To make this more easily understood, let us divide the Church into two principal orders — the clergy and the people. I use the word *clergy* as the common, though improper, appellation of those who execute the public ministry in the Church. We shall, first, speak of the common discipline to which all ought to be subject; and in the next place we shall proceed to the clergy, who, beside this common discipline, have a discipline peculiar to themselves. But as some have such a hatred of discipline, as to abhor the very name, they should attend to the following consideration: That if no society, and even no house, though containing only a small family, can be preserved in a proper state without discipline, this is far more necessary in the Church, the state of which ought to be the most orderly of all. As the saving doctrine of Christ is the soul of the Church, so discipline forms the ligaments which connect the members together, and keep each in its proper place. Whoever, therefore, either desire the abolition of all discipline, or obstruct its restoration, whether they act from design or inadvertency, they certainly promote the entire dissolution of the Church. For what will be the consequence, if every man be at liberty to follow his own inclinations? But such would be the case, unless the preaching of the doctrine were accompanied with private admonitions, reproofs, and other means to enforce the doctrine, and prevent it from being altogether ineffectual. Discipline, therefore, serves as a bridle to curb and restrain the refractory, who resist the doctrine of Christ; or as a spur to stimulate the inactive; and sometimes as a father's rod, with which those who have grievously fallen may be chastised in mercy, and with the gentleness of the Spirit of Christ. . . .

IV. xii. 2   The first foundation of discipline consists in the use of private admonitions; that is to say, that if any one be guilty of a voluntary omission of duty, or conduct himself in an insolent manner, or discover a want of virtue in his life, or commit any act deserving of reprehension, he should suffer himself to be admonished; and that every one should study to admonish his brother, whenever occasion shall require; but that pastors and presbyters, beyond all others, should be vigilant in the discharge of his duty, being called by their office, not only to preach to the congregation, but also to admonish and exhort in private houses, if in any instances their public instructions may not have been sufficiently efficacious.

IV. xii. 3   . . . It is necessary to make this distinction — that some sins are private, and others public or notorious. With respect to the former, Christ says to every private individual, " Tell him his fault between thee and him alone." (e) With respect to those which are notorious, Paul says to Timothy, " Them that sin rebuke before all, that others also may fear." (f) . . . The legitimate course, then will be, — in correcting secret faults, to adopt the different steps directed by Christ; and in the case of those which are notorious, to proceed at once to the solemn correction of the Church, especially

IV. xii. 4   if they be attended with public offence. It is also necessary to make another distinction between different sins; some are smaller delinquencies, others are flagitious or enormous crimes. For the correction of atrocious crimes, it is not sufficient to employ admonition or reproof; recourse must be had to a severer remedy. . . .

IV. xii. 5   Now, there are three ends proposed by the Church in those corrections, and in excommunication. The first is, that those who

---

(e) Matt. xviii. 15.   (f) 1 Tim. v. 20.

lead scandalous and flagitious lives, may not, to the dishonour of God, be numbered among Christians; as if his holy Church were a conspiracy of wicked and abandoned men. . . . Here it is also necessary to have particular regard to the Lord's supper, that it may not be profaned by a promiscuous administration. . . . The second end is, that the good may not be corrupted, as is often the case, by constant association with the wicked. For, such is our propensity to error, nothing is more easy than for evil examples to seduce us from rectitude of conduct. . . . The third end is, that those who are censured or excommunicated, confounded with the shame of their turpitude, may be led to repentance. Thus it is even conducive to their own benefit for their iniquity to be punished, that the stroke of the rod may arouse to a confession of their guilt, those who would only be rendered more obstinate by indulgence. . . .

Having stated these ends, it remains for us to examine how the IV. xii. 6 Church exercises this branch of discipline, which consists in jurisdiction. In the first place, let us keep in view the distinction before mentioned, that some sins are public, and others private, or more concealed. Public sins are those which are not only known to one or two witnesses, but are committed openly, and to the scandal of the whole Church. By private sins, I mean, not such as are entirely unknown to men, like those of hypocrites, — for these never come under the cognizance of the Church, — but those of an intermediate class, which are not without the knowledge of some witnesses, and yet are not public. The first sort requires not the adoption of the gradual measures enumerated by Christ; but it is the duty of the Church, on the occurrence of any notorious scandal, immediately to summon the offender, and to punish him in proportion to his crime. Sins of the second class, according to the rule of Christ, are not to be brought before the Church, unless they are attended with contumacy, in rejecting private admonition. When they are submitted to the cognizance of the Church, then attention is to be paid to the other distinction, between smaller delinquencies and more atrocious crimes. For slighter offences require not the exertion of extreme severity; it is sufficient to administer verbal castigation, and that with paternal gentleness, not calculated to exasperate or confound the offender, but to bring him to himself, that his correction may be an occasion of joy rather than of sorrow. But it is proper that flagitious crimes should receive severer punishment; for it is not enough for him who has grievously offended the Church by the bad example of an atrocious crime, merely to receive verbal castigation; he ought to be deprived of the communion of the Lord's supper for a time, till he shall have given satisfactory evidence of repentence. . . .

IV. xii. 7   The legitimate process in excommunicating an offender, which is pointed out by Paul, requires it to be done, not by the elders alone, but with the knowledge and approbation of the Church: in such a manner, however, that the multitude of the people may not direct the proceeding, but may watch over it as witnesses and guardians, that nothing may be done by a few persons from any improper motive. Beside the invocation of the name of God, the whole of the proceeding ought to be conducted with a gravity declarative of the presence of Christ, that there may be no doubt of his presiding over the sentence.

IV. xii. 8   But it ought not to be forgotten, that the severity becoming the Church must be tempered with a spirit of gentleness. . . . When the sinner gives the Church a testimony of his repentance, and by this testimony, as far as in him lies, obliterates the offence, he is by no means to be pressed any further; and if he be pressed any

IV. xii. 9   further, the rigour is carried beyond its proper limits. . . . To comprehend all in a word, let us not condemn to eternal death the person himself, who is in the hand and power of God alone, but let us content ourselves with judging of the nature of his works according to the law of the Lord. . . .

IV. xii. 14   The remaining part of discipline . . . consists in this — that the pastors, according to the necessity of the times, should exhort the people either to fastings or solemn supplications, or to other exercises of humility, repentance, and faith, of which the word of God prescribes neither the time, the extent, nor the form, but leaves all this to the judgment of the Church. . . . Whenever a controversy arises respecting religion, which requires to be decided by a council or ecclesiastical judgment; whenever a minister is to be chosen; in short, whenever any thing of difficulty or great importance is transacting; and also when any tokens of the Divine wrath are discovered, such as famine, pestilence, or war; — it is a

pious custom, and beneficial in all ages, for the pastors to exhort
the people to public fasts and extraordinary prayers. . . .

There remains the second part of the discipline of the Church, **IV. xii. 22**
which particularly relates to the clergy. It is contained in the
canons which the ancient bishops imposed on themselves and their
order; such as these: That no ecclesiastic should employ his time
in hunting, gambling, or feasting; that no one should engage in
usury or commerce; that no one should be present at dissolute
dances; and other similar injunctions. Penalties were likewise annexed, to confirm the authority of the canons, and to prevent their
being violated with impunity. For this end, to every bishop was
committed the government of his clergy, to rule them according to
the canons, and to oblige them to do their duty. For this purpose
were instituted annual visitations and synods, that if any one were
negligent in his duty, he might be admonished, and that any one
who committed a fault might be corrected according to his offence.
The bishops also had their provincial councils, once every year,
and anciently even twice a year, by which they were judged, if they
had committed any breach of their duty. For if a bishop was too
severe or violent against his clergy, there was a right of appeal to
the provincial councils, even though there was only a single com-
plainant. The severest punishment was the deposition of the offender from his office, and his exclusion for a time from the communion. And because this was a perpetual regulation, they never
used to dissolve a provincial council without appointing a time
and place for the next. For, to summon a universal council, was
the exclusive prerogative of the emperor, as all the ancient records
testify. As long as his severity continued, the clergy required
nothing more from the people than they exemplified in their own
conduct. Indeed, they were far more severe to themselves than to
the laity; and it is reasonable that the people should be ruled with
a milder and less rigid discipline; and that the clergy should inflict
heavier censures, and exercise far less indulgence to themselves
than to other persons. How all this has become obsolete, it is unnecessary to relate. . . . In one instance, they are too rigorous
and inflexible, that is, in not permitting priests to marry. . . . In   **IV. xii. 23**
the first place, it was on no account lawful for men to prohibit
that which the Lord had left free. Secondly, that God had expressly

IV. xii. 24

provided in his word that this liberty should not be infringed, is too clear to require much proof. . . . Christ has been pleased to put such honour upon marriage, as to make it an image of his sacred union with the Church. What could be said more, in commendation of the dignity of marriage? . . .

CHAPTER XXIV

The Sacraments

(1) THE NATURE AND PURPOSE
OF THE SACRAMENTS

Connected with the preaching of the gospel, another assistance and support for our faith is presented to us in the sacraments; on the subject of which it is highly important to lay down some certain doctrine, that we may learn for what end they were instituted, and how they ought to be used. In the first place, it is necessary to consider what a sacrament is. Now, I think it will be a simple and appropriate definition, if we say that it is an outward sign, by which the Lord seals in our consciences the promises of his good-will towards us, to support the weakness of our faith; and we on our part testify our piety towards him, in his presence and that of angels, as well as before men. It may, however, be more briefly defined, in other words, by calling it a testimony of the grace of God towards us, confirmed by an outward sign, with a reciprocal attestation of our piety towards him. Whichever of these definitions be chosen, it conveys exactly the same meaning as that of Augustine, which states a sacrament to be " a visible sign of a sacred thing," or " a visible form of invisible grace." . . .

Now, from the definition which we have established, we see that there is never any sacrament without an antecedent promise of God, to which it is subjoined as an appendix, in order to confirm and seal the promise itself, and to certify and ratify it to us; which means God foresees to be necessary, in the first place on account of our ignorance and dulness, and in the next place on account of our weakness; and yet, strictly speaking, not so much for the confirmation of his sacred word, as for our establishment in the faith of it. For the truth of God is sufficiently solid and certain in itself, and can receive no better confirmation from any other quarter than from itself; but our faith being slender and weak, unless it be supported on every side, and sustained by every assistance, immediately shakes, fluctuates, totters, and falls. And as we are corporeal, always creeping on the ground, cleaving to terrestrial and carnal objects, and incapable of understanding or conceiving of any thing of a spiritual nature, our merciful Lord, in his infinite indulgence, accommodates himself to our capacity, condescending to lead us to himself even by these earthly elements, and in the flesh itself to present to us a mirror of spiritual blessings. . . .

IV. xiv. 9   With respect to the confirmation and increase of faith . . . I wish the reader to be apprized, . . . that I assign this office to the sacraments; not from an opinion of their possessing a perpetual inherent virtue, efficacious of itself to the advancement or confirmation of faith; but because they have been instituted by the Lord for the express purpose of promoting its establishment and augumentation. But they only perform their office aright when they are accompanied by the Spirit, that internal Teacher, by whose energy alone our hearts are penetrated, our affections are moved, and an entrance is opened for the sacraments into our souls. If he be absent, the sacraments can produce no more effect upon our minds than the splendour of the sun on blind eyes, or the sound of a voice on deaf ears. I make such a distinction and distribution, therefore, between the Spirit and the sacraments, that I consider all the energy of operation as belonging to the Spirit, and the sacraments as mere instruments, which, without his agency, are vain and useless, but which, when he acts and exerts his power in the heart, are fraught with surprising efficacy. Now, it is evident how, according to this opinion, the faith of a pious mind is confirmed by the sacraments; namely, as the eyes see by the light of the sun, and the ears hear by the sound of a voice: the light would have no effect upon the eyes, unless they had a natural faculty capable of being enlightened; and it would be in vain for the ears to be struck with any sound, if they had not been naturally formed for hearing. But if it be true, as we ought at once to conclude, that what the visive faculty is in our eyes towards our beholding the light, and the faculty of hearing is in our ears towards our perception of sound, such is the work of the Holy Spirit in our hearts for the formation, support, preservation, and establishment of our faith; then these two consequences immediately follow — that the sacraments are attended with no benefit without the influence of the Holy Spirit; and that, in hearts already instructed by that Teacher, they still subserve the confirmation and increase of faith. There is only this difference that our eyes and ears are naturally endued with the faculties of seeing and hearing, but Christ accomplishes this in our hearts by special and preternatural grace. . . .

Let us abide by this conclusion, that the office of the sacraments **IV. xiv. 17** is precisely the same as that of the word of God; which is to offer and present Christ to us, and in him the treasures of his heavenly grace; but they confer no advantage or profit without being received by faith; just as wine, or oil, or any other liquor, though it be poured plentifully on a vessel, yet will it overflow and be lost, unless the mouth of the vessel be open; and the vessel itself, though wet on the outside, will remain dry and empty within. . . . The sacraments . . . fulfil to us, on the part of God, the same office as messengers of joyful intelligence, or earnests for the confirmation of covenants on the part of men; they communicate no grace from themselves, but announce and show, and, as earnests and pledges, ratify, the things which are given to us by the goodness of God. The Holy Spirit, whom the sacraments do not promiscuously impart to all but whom God, by a peculiar privilege, confers upon his servants, is he who brings with him the graces of God, who gives the sacraments admission into our hearts, and causes them to bring forth fruit in us. . . .

The sacraments have been different according to the varieties **IV. xiv. 20** of different periods, and corresponding to the dispensation by which it has pleased the Lord to manifest himself in different ways to mankind. For to Abraham and his posterity circumcision was commanded; to which the law of Moses afterwards added ablutions, sacrifices, and other rites. These were the sacraments of the Jews till the coming of Christ; which was followed by the abrogation of these, and the institution of two others, which are now used in the Christian Church; namely, baptism and the supper of the Lord. . . . Those ancient sacrifices . . . referred to the same object towards which ours are now directed, their design being to point and lead to Christ, or rather, as images, to represent and make him known. For as we have already shown that they are seals to confirm the promises of God, and it is very certain that no promise of God was ever offered to man except in Christ, — in order to teach us any thing respecting the promises of God, they must of necessity make a discovery of Christ. . . . There is only one difference between those sacraments and ours: they prefigured Christ as promised and still expected; ours represent him as already come and manifested. . . .

IV. xiv. 22   Our two sacraments present us with a clearer exhibition of Christ, in proportion to the nearer view of him which men have enjoyed since he was really manifested by the Father in the manner in which he had been promised. For baptism testifies to us our purgation and ablution; the eucharistic supper testifies our redemption. Water is a figure of ablution, and blood of satisfaction. . . . In the water and the blood we have a testimony of purgation and redemption; and the Spirit, as the principal witness, confirms and secures our reception and belief of this testimony. . . .

(2) BAPTISM

IV. xv. 1   Baptism is a sign of initiation, by which we are admitted into the society of the Church, in order that, being incorporated into Christ, we may be numbered among the children of God. Now, it has been given to us by God for these ends, which I have shown to be common to all sacraments: first, to promote our faith towards him; secondly, to testify our confession before men. We shall treat of both these ends of its institution in order. To begin with the first: from baptism our faith derives three advantages, which require to be distinctly considered. The first is, that it is proposed to us by the Lord, as a symbol and token of our purification; or, to express my meaning more fully, it resembles a legal instrument properly attested, by which he assures us that all our sins are cancelled, effaced, and obliterated, so that they will never appear in his sight, or come into his remembrance, or be imputed to us. For he commands all who believe to be baptized for the remission of their sins. Therefore those who have imagined that baptism is nothing more than a mark or sign by which we profess our religion before men, as soldiers wear the insignia of their sovereign as a mark of their profession, have not considered that which was the principal thing in baptism; which is, that we ought to receive it with this promise, " He that believeth and is baptized shall be saved." (t) . . . But . . . baptism promises us no other   IV. xv. 2 purification than by the sprinkling of the blood of Christ; which is emblematically represented by water, on account of its resemblance to washing and cleansing. Who, then, can pretend that we are cleansed by that water, which clearly testifies the blood of Christ to be our true and only ablution? So that, to refute the error of those who refer all to the virtue of the water, no better argument could be found, than in the signification of baptism itself, which abstracts us, as well from that visible element which is placed before our eyes, as from all other means of salvation, that it may fix our minds on Christ alone.

Nor must it be supposed that baptism is administered only for   IV. xv. 3 the time past, so that for sins into which we fall after baptism it would be necessary to seek other new remedies of expiation in I know not what other sacraments, as if the virtue of baptism were become obsolete. . . . At whatever time we are baptized, we are washed and purified for the whole of life. . . . Now, from this doctrine we ought not to take a license for the commission of future sins; for it is very far from inculcating such presumption; it is only delivered to those who, when they have sinned, groan under the fatigue and oppression of their transgressions; in order to afford them some relief and consolation, and to preserve them from sinking into confusion and despair. . . .

Baptism is also attended with another advantage: it shows us   IV. xv. 5 our mortification in Christ, and our new life in him. For, as the apostle says, " So many of us as were baptized into Jesus Christ,

---

(t) Mark xvi. 16.

were baptized into his death: therefore we are buried with him by baptism into death, that we should walk in newness of life." (*y*) In this passage he does not merely exhort us to an imitation of Christ, as if he had said, that we are admonished by baptism, that after the example of his death we should die to sin, and that after the example of his resurrection we should rise to righteousness; but he goes considerably further, and teaches us, that by baptism Christ has made us partakers of his death, in order that we may be ingrafted into it. . . . Thus we are promised, first, the gratuitous remission of sins, and imputation of righteousness; and, secondly, the grace of the Holy Spirit to reform us to newness of life.

IV. xv. 6   The last advantage which our faith receives from baptism, is the certain testimony it affords us, that we are not only ingrafted into the life and death of Christ, but are so united as to be partakers of all his benefits. For this reason he dedicated and sanctified baptism in his own body, that he might have it in common with us, as a most firm bond of the union and society which he has condescended to form with us; so that Paul proves from it, that we are the children of God, because we have put on Christ in baptism. (*c*) Thus we see that the accomplishment of baptism is in Christ; whom, on this account, we call the proper object of baptism. Therefore it is no wonder if the apostles baptized in his name, (*d*) though they had also been commanded to baptize in the name of the Father and of the Spirit. (*e*) For all the gifts of God, which are presented in baptism, are found in Christ alone. Yet it cannot be but that he who baptizes into Christ, equally invokes the name of the Father and of the Spirit. For we have purification in his blood, because our merciful Father, in his incomparable goodness, being pleased to receive us to his mercy, has appointed this Mediator between us, to conciliate his favour to us. But we receive regeneration from his death and resurrection, when we are endued with a new and spiritual nature by the sanctification of the Spirit. Of our purification and regeneration, therefore, we obtain, and distinctly perceive, the cause in the Father, the matter in the Son, and the efficacy in the Spirit. . . .

(*y*) Rom. vi. 3, 4.   (*c*) Gal. iii. 26, 27.
(*d*) Acts viii. 16.   (*e*) Matt. xxviii. 19.

Now, we . . . clearly perceive the falsehood of the notion . . .   IV. xv. 10
— that by baptism we are delivered and exempted from original
sin, and from the corruption which has descended from Adam to
all his posterity, and are restored to the same righteousness and
purity of nature which Adam would have obtained if he had continued in the integrity in which he was first created. For teachers
of this kind have never understood the nature of original sin, or
original righteousness, or the grace of baptism. Now, we have
already proved that original sin is the pravity and corruption of
our nature, which first renders us obnoxious to the wrath of God,
and then produces in us those works which the Scripture calls
" works of the flesh." (o) Therefore these two things are to be distinctly observed: first, that our nature being so entirely depraved
and vitiated, we are, on account of this very corruption, considered
as convicted and justly condemned in the sight of God, to whom
nothing is acceptable but righteousness, innocence, and purity.
And therefore even infants themselves bring their own condemnation into the world with them, who, though they have not yet produced the fruits of their iniquity, yet have the seed of it within
them; even their whole nature is, as it were, a seed of sin, and
therefore cannot but be odious and abominable to God. By baptism, believers are certified that this condemnation is removed
from them; since, as we said, the Lord promises us by this sign,
that a full and entire remission is granted both of the guilt which
is to be imputed to us, and of the punishment to be inflicted on
account of that guilt; they also receive righteousness, such as the
people of God may obtain in this life; that is, only by imputation, because the Lord, in his mercy, accepts them as righteous
and innocent.

The other thing to be remarked is, that this depravity never   IV. xv. 11
ceases in us, but is perpetually producing new fruits — those
works of the flesh which we have already described, like the emis-
sion of flame and sparks from a heated furnace, or like the streams
of water from an unfailing spring. For concupiscence never dies,
nor is altogether extinguished in men, till by death they are delivered from the body of death, and entirely divested of themselves.

(o) Gal. v. 19.

Baptism, indeed, promises us the submersion of our Pharaoh, and the mortification of sin; yet not so that it no longer exists, or gives us no further trouble; but only that it may never overcome us. For as long as we live immured in this prison of the body, the relics of sin will dwell in us; but if we hold fast by faith the promise which God has given us in baptism, they shall not domineer or reign over us. But let no one deceive himself, let no one flatter himself in his guilt, when he hears that sin always dwells in us. These things are not said in order that those who are already too prone to do evil may securely sleep in their sins, but only that those who are tempted by their corrupt propensities may not faint and sink into despondency; but that they may rather reflect that they are yet in the way, and may consider themselves as having made some progress, when they experience their corruptions diminishing from day to day, till they shall attain the mark at which they are aiming, even the final destruction of their depravity, which will be accomplished at the close of this mortal life. In the mean time, let them not cease to fight manfully, to animate themselves to constant advances, and to press forward to complete victory. For it ought to give additional impulse to their exertions, to see that, after they have been striving so long, so much still remains for them to do. We conclude, therefore, that we are baptized into the mortification of the flesh, which commences in us at baptism, which we pursue from day to day, and which will be perfected when we shall pass out of this life to the Lord. . . .

IV. xv. 13   Baptism also serves for our confession before men. For it is a mark by which we openly profess our desire to be numbered among the people of God, by which we testify our agreement with all Christians in the worship of one God, and in one religion, and by which we make a public declaration of our faith; that the praises of God may not only be breathed in the secret aspirations of our hearts, but may also be loudly proclaimed by our tongues, and by all the members of our body, in the different modes in which they are capable of expressing them. For thus all that we have is devoted, as it ought to be, to the glory of God, to which every thing ought to be subservient, and by our example others are incited to the same pursuit. It was with this view that Paul inquired of the Corinthians, whether they had not been baptized in the name of

Christ; signifying that, in having been baptized in his name, they had dedicated themselves to him, had avowed him as their Lord and Master, and had bound themselves by a solemn obligation before men; so that they could never again confess any other except him, unless they intended to renounce the confession which they had made at their baptism. . . .

From this sacrament, as from all others, we obtain nothing except what we receive by faith. If faith be wanting, it will be a testimony of our ingratitude, to render us guilty before God, because we have not believed the promise given in the sacrament; but as baptism is a sign of our confession, we ought to testify by it, that our confidence is in the mercy of God, and our purity in the remission of sins, which is obtained for us by Jesus Christ; and that we enter into the Church of God in order to live in the same harmony of faith and charity, of one mind with all the faithful. This is what Paul meant when he said, that "by one Spirit we are all baptized into one body." (s) . . . *IV. xv. 15*

With respect to the external symbol [of this mystery], I sincerely wish that the genuine institution of Christ had the influence it ought to have, to repress the audacity of man. . . . It is lawful for me and for all believers to reject every thing that men have presumed to add to the institution of Christ. . . . How much better was it, therefore, omitting all theatrical pomps which dazzle the eyes and stupefy the minds of the simple, whenever any one was to be baptized, that he should be presented to the congregation of believers, and be offered to God in the presence and with the prayers of the whole Church; that the confession of faith, in which the catechumen was to be instructed, should be recited; that the promises which are included in baptism should be declared; that the catechumen should be baptized in the name of the Father, of the Son, and of the Holy Ghost; and lastly, that he should be dismissed with prayers and thanksgivings! Thus nothing material would be omitted; and that one ceremony, which was instituted by God, would shine with the greatest lustre, unencumbered with any extraneous corruptions. But whether the person who is baptized be wholly immersed, and whether thrice or *IV. xv. 19*

(s) 1 Cor. xii. 13.

once, or whether water be only poured or sprinkled upon him, is of no importance; Churches ought to be left at liberty, in this respect, to act according to the difference of countries. The very word *baptize*, however, signifies to immerse; and it is certain that immersion was the practice of the ancient Church.

IV. xv. 20   It is also necessary to state, that it is not right for private persons to take upon themselves the administration of baptism; for this, as well as the administration of the Lord's supper, is a part of the public ministry of the Church. Christ never commanded women, or men in general, to baptize; he gave this charge to those whom he had appointed to be apostles. . . . But it is alleged, there is danger, lest a child, who is sick and dies without baptism, should be deprived of the grace of regeneration. This I can by no means admit. God pronounces that he adopts our infants as his children, before they are born, when he promises that he will be a God to us, and to our seed after us. This promise includes their

IV. xv. 22   salvation. . . . Infants are not excluded from the kingdom of heaven, who happen to die before they have had the privilege of baptism. . . . The sacrament is afterwards added as a seal, not to give efficacy to the promise of God, as if it wanted validity in itself, but only to confirm it to us. Whence it follows, that the children of believers are not baptized, that they may thereby be made the children of God, as if they had before been strangers to the Church; but, on the contrary, they are received into the Church by a solemn sign, because they already belonged to the body of Christ by virtue of the promise. If the omission of the sign, therefore, be not occasioned by indolence, or contempt, or negligence, we are safe from all danger. It is far more consistent with piety to show this reverence to the institution of God, not to receive the sacraments from any other hands than those to which the Lord has committed them. When it is impossible to receive them from the Church, the grace of God is not so attached to them, but that we may obtain it by faith from the word of the Lord. . . .

(3) THE LORD'S SUPPER

IV. xvii. 1   After God has once received us into his family, and not only so as to admit us among his servants, but to number us with his children, — in order to fulfil the part of a most excellent father, solicitous for his offspring, he also undertakes to sustain and nourish us as long as we live; and not content with this, he has been pleased to give us a pledge, as a further assurance of this neverceasing liberality. For this purpose, therefore, by the hand of his only begotten Son, he has favoured his Church with another sacrament, a spiritual banquet, in which Christ testifies himself to be the bread of life, to feed our souls for a true and blessed immortality. . . . The signs are bread and wine, which represent to us the invisible nourishment which we receive from the body and blood of Christ. For as in baptism God regenerates us, incorporates us into the society of his Church, and makes us his children by adoption, so we have said, that he acts towards us the part of a provident father of a family, in constantly supplying us with food, to sustain and preserve us in that life to which he has begotten us by his word. Now, the only food of our souls is Christ; and to him, therefore, our heavenly Father invites us, that being refreshed by a participation of him, we may gain fresh vigour from day to day, till we arrive at the heavenly immortality. And because this mystery of the secret union of Christ with believers is incomprehensible by nature, he exhibits a figure and image of it in visible signs, peculiarly adapted to our feeble capacity; and, as it were, by giving tokens and pledges, renders it equally as certain to us as if we beheld it with our eyes; for the dullest minds understand this very familiar similitude, that our souls are nourished by Christ, just as the life of the body is supported by bread and wine. We see, then, for what end this mystical benediction is designed; namely, to assure us that the body of the Lord was once offered as a sacrifice for us, so that we may now feed upon it, and, feeding on it, may experience within us the efficacy of that one sacrifice; and that his blood was once shed for us, so that it is our perpetual drink. And this is the import of the words of the promise annexed to it: "Take, eat; this is my body, which is given for you." The body, therefore, which was once offered for our salvation, we are commanded to take and eat; that seeing ourselves made partakers of it, we may certainly conclude, that the virtue of that life-giving death will be efficacious within us. Hence, also, he calls the cup "the new testament," or rather *covenant*, in his blood. (d) For the covenant which he once ratified with his blood, he in some measure renews, or rather continues, as far as relates to the confirmation of our faith, whenever he presents us that sacred blood to drink.

IV. xvii. 2   From this sacrament pious souls may derive the benefit of considerable satisfaction and confidence; because it affords us a testimony that we are incorporated into one body with Christ, so that whatever is his, we are at liberty to call ours. The consequence of this is, that we venture to assure ourselves of our interest in eternal life, of which he is the heir, and that the kingdom of heaven, into which he has already entered, can no more be lost by us than by him; and, on the other hand, that we cannot be condemned by our sins, from the guilt of which he absolved us, when he wished them to be imputed to himself, as if they were his own. This is the wonderful exchange which, in his infinite goodness, he has made with us. Submitting to our poverty, he has transferred to us his riches; assuming our weakness, he has strengthened us by his power; accepting our mortality, he has conferred on us his immortality; taking on himself the load of iniquity with which we were oppressed, he has clothed us with his righteousness; descending to the earth, he has prepared a way for our ascending to heaven; becoming with us the Son of man, he has made us, with himself, the sons of God.

IV. xvii. 3   Of all these things we have such a complete attestation in this sacrament, that we may confidently consider them as truly exhibited to us, as if Christ himself were presented to our eyes, and touched by our hands. For there can be no falsehood or illusion in this word, "Take, eat, drink; this is my body which is given for you; this is my blood which is shed for the remission of sins." By commanding us to take, he signifies that he is ours; by commanding us to eat and drink, he signifies that he is become one substance with us. In saying that his body is given for us, and his blood shed for us, he shows that both are not so much his as ours, because he assumed and laid down both, not for his own advantage, but for our salvation. And it ought to be carefully observed, that the principal and almost entire energy of the sacrament lies in

---

(d) Matt. xxvi. 26, 28.   Mark xiv. 22, 24.   Luke xxii. 19, 20.   1 Cor. xi. 24, 25.

these words, " which is given for you; " " which is shed for you; "
for otherwise it would avail us but little, that the body and blood
of the Lord are distributed to us now, if they had not been once
delivered for our redemption and salvation. Therefore they are
represented to us by bread and wine, to teach us that they are not
only ours, but are destined for the support of our spiritual life.
This is what we have already suggested — that by the corporeal
objects which are presented in the sacrament, we are conducted,
by a kind of analogy, to those which are spiritual. So, when bread
is given to us as a symbol of the body of Christ, we ought immediately to conceive of this comparison, that, as bread nourishes,
sustains, and preserves the life of the body, so the body of Christ
is the only food to animate and support the life of the soul. When
we see wine presented as a symbol of his blood, we ought to think
of the uses of wine to the human body, that we may contemplate
the same advantages conferred upon us in a spiritual manner by
the blood of Christ; which are these — that it nourishes, refreshes,
strengthens, and exhilarates. For if we duly consider the benefits
resulting to us from the oblation of his sacred body, and the effusion of his blood, we shall clearly perceive that these properties
of bread and wine, according to this analogy, are most justly attributed to those symbols, as administered to us in the Lord's
supper. . . .

The sacrament . . . does not first constitute Christ the bread   IV. xvii. 5
of life; but, by recalling to our remembrance that he has been
made the bread of life, upon which we may constantly feed, and
by giving us a taste and relish for that bread, it causes us to experience the support which it is adapted to afford. For it assures
us, in the first place, that whatever Christ has done or suffered,
was for the purpose of giving life to us; and, in the next place,
that this life will never end. . . . He gave [his body] . . . to be
made bread, when he surrendered it to be crucified for the redemption of the world; he gives it daily, when, by the word of the
gospel, he presents it to us, that we may partake of it as crucified;
when he confirms that presentation by the sacred mystery of the
supper; when he accomplishes within that which he signifies
without. Here it behoves us to guard against two errors; that, on
the one hand, we may not, by undervaluing the signs, disjoin them

from the mysteries with which they are connected; nor, on the other hand, by extolling them beyond measure, obscure the glory of the mysteries themselves. . . .

IV. xvii. 11   The sacred mystery of the supper consists of two parts: the corporeal signs, which, being placed before our eyes, represent to us invisible things in a manner adapted to the weakness of our capacities; and the spiritual truth, which is at the same time typified and exhibited by those symbols. When I intend to give a familiar view of this truth, I am accustomed to state three particulars which it includes: the signification; the matter, or substance, which depends on the signification; and the virtue, or effect, which follows from both. The signification consists in the promises which are interwoven with the sign. What I call the matter or substance, is Christ, with his death and resurrection. By the effect, I mean redemption, righteousness, sanctification, eternal life, and all the other benefits which Christ confers upon us. . . . In the mystery of the supper, under the symbols of the bread and wine, Christ is truly exhibited to us, even his body and blood, in which he has fulfilled all obedience to procure our justification. And the design of this exhibition is, first, that we may be united into one body with him, and, secondly, that being made partakers of his substance, we may experience his power in the communication of all blessings. . . .

IV. xvii. 19   It is necessary for us to establish such a presence of Christ in the sacred supper, as neither, on the one hand, to fasten him to the element of bread, or to enclose him in it, or in any way to circumscribe him, which would derogate from his celestial glory; nor, on the other hand, to deprive him of his corporeal dimensions, or to represent his body as in different places at once, or to assign it an immensity diffused through heaven and earth, which would be clearly inconsistent with the reality of his human nature. Let us never suffer ourselves to be driven from these two exceptions; that nothing be maintained derogatory to Christ's celestial glory; which is the case when he is represented as brought under the corruptible elements of this world, or fastened to any earthly objects; and that nothing be attributed to his body incompatible with the human nature; which is the case when it is represented as infinite, or is said to be in more places than one at the same time. . . .

The account [of the institution itself] given by three of the IV. xvii. 20 evangelists, and by Paul, informs us, that " Jesus took bread, and gave thanks, and blessed it, and brake it, and gave it to the disciples, and said, Take, eat; this is my body, which is given or broken for you. And he took the cup, and said, This cup is my blood of the new testament, or the new testament in my blood, which is shed for you, and for many, for the remission of sins." (h) The advocates of transubstantiation contend that the pronoun *this* denotes the appearance of the bread, because the consecration is made by the whole of the sentence, and there is no visible substance, according to them, which can be indicated by it. . . . Those of them who express themselves more modestly, though they strenuously insist on the literal meaning of these words, " *This is my body*," yet afterwards depart from their literal precision, and explain them to import that the body of Christ is with the bread, in the bread, and under the bread. . . .

They are exceedingly deceived, who cannot conceive of any IV. xvii. 31 presence of the flesh of Christ in the supper, except it be attached to the bread. For on this principle they leave nothing to the secret operation of the Spirit, which unites us to Christ. They suppose Christ not to be present, unless he descends to us; as though we cannot equally enjoy his presence, if he elevates us to himself. The only question between us, therefore, respects the manner of this presence; because they place Christ in the bread, and we think it unlawful for us to bring him down from heaven. Let the readers judge on which side the truth lies. Only let us hear no more of that calumny, that Christ is excluded from the sacrament, unless he be concealed under the bread. For as this is a heavenly mystery, there is no necessity to bring Christ down to the earth, in order to be united to us.

If any one inquire of me respecting the manner, I shall not be IV. xvii. 32 ashamed to acknowledge, that it is a mystery too sublime for me to be able to express, or even to comprehend; and, to be still more explicit, I rather experience it, than understand it. Here, therefore, without any controversy, I embrace the truth of God, on which I can safely rely. He pronounces his flesh to be the food and

(h) Matt. xxvi. 26—28. Mark. xiv. 22—24. Luke xxii. 19, 20. 1 Cor. xi. 23—25.

his blood the drink, of my soul. I offer him my soul, to be nourished with such aliment. In his sacred supper, he commands me, under the symbols of bread and wine, to take, and eat, and drink, his body and blood. I doubt not that he truly presents, and that I receive them. . . . The presence of Christ's body . . . is such as the nature of the sacrament requires; where we affirm that it appears with so much virtue and efficacy, as not only to afford our minds an undoubted confidence of eternal life, but also to give us an assurance of the resurrection and immortality of our bodies. For they are vivified by his immortal flesh, and in some degree participate his immortality. . . .

IV. xvii. 43   With respect to the external ceremonial, whether believers take the bread in their hands or not; whether they divide it between them, or every individual eat that which is given to him; whether they return the cup into the hand of the deacon, or deliver it to the person who is next; whether the bread be leavened or unleavened; whether the wine be red or white; is not of the least importance. These things are indifferent, and left to the liberty of the Church. . . .

The Lord's supper might be most properly administered, if it were set before the Church very frequently, and at least once in every week in the following manner: The service should commence with public prayer; in the next place, a sermon should be delivered; then, the bread and wine being placed upon the table, the minister should recite the institution of the supper, should declare the promises which are left to us in it, and, at the same time, should excommunicate all those who are excluded from it by the prohibition of the Lord; after this, prayer should be offered, that with the same benignity with which our Lord has given us this sacred food, he would also teach and enable us to receive it in faith and gratitude of heart, and that, as of ourselves we are not worthy, he would, in his mercy, make us worthy of such a feast. Then either some psalms should be sung, or a portion of Scripture should be read, and believers, in a becoming order, should participate of the sacred banquet, the ministers breaking the bread and distributing it, and presenting the cup, to the people; after the conclusion of the supper, an exhortation should be given to sincere faith, and a confession of the same; to charity, and a deportment worthy of

Christians. Finally, thanksgivings should be rendered, and praises sung, to God; and to close the whole, the Church should be dismissed in peace. . . .

The readers may now see, collected into a brief summary, almost every thing that I have thought important to be known respecting these two sacraments; the use of which has been enjoined on the Christian Church from the commencement of the New Testament until the end of time; that is to say, baptism, to be a kind of entrance into the Church, and an initiatory profession of faith; and the Lord's supper, to be a continual nourishment, with which Christ spiritually feeds his family of believers. Wherefore, as there is but " one God, one Christ, one faith," one Church, the body of Christ, so there is only " one baptism " and that is never repeated; but the supper is frequently distributed, that those who have once been admitted into the Church, may understand that they are continually nourished by Christ. Beside these two, as no other sacrament has been instituted by God, so no other ought to be acknowledged by the Church of believers. For that it is not left to the will of man to institute new sacraments, will be easily understood if we remember what has already been very plainly stated — that sacraments are appointed by God for the purpose of instructing us respecting some promise of his, and assuring us of his good-will towards us; and if we also consider, that no one has been the counsellor of God, capable of affording us any certainty respecting his will, (c) or furnishing us any assurance of his disposition towards us, what he chooses to give or to deny us. Hence it follows, that no one can institute a sign to be a testimony respecting any determination or promise of his; he alone can furnish us a testimony respecting himself by giving a sign. I will express myself in terms more concise, and perhaps more homely, but more explicit — that there can be no sacrament unaccompanied with a promise of salvation. All mankind, collected in one assembly, can promise us nothing respecting our salvation. Therefore they can never institute or establish a sacrament. . . .

IV. xviii. 19

(c) Isaiah xl. 14.   Rom. xi. 34.

CHAPTER XXV

The Church and the State

❧

(1) SPIRITUAL AND CIVIL GOVERNMENT

HAVING already stated that man is the subject of two kinds of government, and having sufficiently discussed that which is situated in the soul, or the inner man, and relates to eternal life, — we are, in this chapter, to say something of the other kind, which relates to civil justice, and the regulation of the external conduct. For, though the nature of this argument seems to have no connection with the spiritual doctrine of faith which I have undertaken to discuss, the sequel will show that I have sufficient reason for connecting them together, and, indeed, that necessity obliges me to it; especially since, on the one hand, infatuated and barbarous men madly endeavour to subvert this ordinance established by God; and, on the other hand, the flatterers of princes, extolling their power beyond all just bounds, hesitate not to oppose it to the authority of God himself. Unless both these errors be resisted, the purity of the faith will be destroyed. . . .

Some men, when they hear that the gospel promises a liberty which acknowledges no king or magistrate among men, but submits to Christ alone, think they can enjoy no advantage of their liberty, while they see any power exalted above them. They imagine, therefore, that nothing will prosper, unless the whole world be modelled in a new form, without any tribunals, or laws, or

202

magistrates, or any thing of a similar kind, which they consider injurious to their liberty. But he who knows how to distinguish between the body and the soul, between this present transitory.life and the future eternal one, will find no difficulty in understanding, that the spiritual kingdom of Christ and civil government are things very different and remote from each other. . . .

Yet this distinction does not lead us to consider the whole sys-   IV. xx. 2
tem of civil government as a polluted thing, which has nothing to do with Christian men. Some fanatics, who are pleased with nothing but liberty, or rather licentiousness without any restraint, do indeed boast and vociferate, That since we are dead with Christ to the elements of this world, and, being translated into the kingdom of God, sit among the celestials, it is a degradation to us, and far beneath our dignity, to be occupied with those secular and impure cares which relate to things altogether uninteresting to a Christian man. Of what use, they ask, are laws without judgments and tribunals? But what have judgments to do with a Christian man? And if it be unlawful to kill, of what use are laws and judgments to us? But as we have just suggested that this kind of government is distinct from that spiritual and internal reign of Christ, so it ought to be known that they are in no respect at variance with each other. For that spiritual reign, even now upon earth, commences within us some preludes of the heavenly kingdom, and in this mortal and transitory life affords us some prelibations of immortal and incorruptible blessedness; but this civil government is designed, as long as we live in this world, to cherish and support the external worship of God, to preserve the pure doctrine of religion, to defend the constitution of the Church, to regulate our lives in a manner requisite for the society of men, to form our manners to civil justice, to promote our concord with each other, and to establish general peace and tranquillity; all which I confess to be superfluous, if the kingdom of God, as it now exists in us, extinguishes the present life. But if it is the will of God, that while we are aspiring towards our true country, we be pilgrims on the earth, and if such aids are necessary to our pilgrimage, they who take them from man deprive him of his human nature. They plead that there should be so much perfection in the Church of God, that its order would suffice to supply the place of all laws; but

they foolishly imagine a perfection which can never be found in any community of men. For since the insolence of the wicked is so great, and their iniquity so obstinate that it can scarcely be restrained by all the severity of the laws, what may we expect they would do, if they found themselves at liberty to perpetrate crimes with impunity, whose outrages even the arm of power cannot altogether prevent? . . .

IV. xx. 3   The exercise of civil polity . . . is equally as necessary to mankind as bread and water, light and air, and far more excellent. For it not only tends to secure the accommodations arising from all these things, that men may breathe, eat, drink, and be sustained in life, though it comprehends all these things while it causes them to live together, yet, I say, this is not its only tendency; its objects also are, that idolatry, sacrileges against the name of God, blasphemies against his truth, and other offences against religion, may not openly appear and be disseminated among the people; that the public tranquillity may not be disturbed; that every person may enjoy his property without molestation; that men may transact their business together without fraud or injustice; that integrity and modesty may be cultivated among them; in short, that there may be a public form of religion among Christians, and that humanity may be maintained among men. Nor let any one think it strange that I now refer to human polity the charge of the due maintenance of religion, which I may appear to have placed beyond the jurisdiction of men. For I do not allow men to make laws respecting religion and the worship of God now, any more than I did before; though I approve of civil government, which provides that the true religion which is contained in the law of God, be not violated, and polluted by public blasphemies, with impunity. But the perspicuity of order will assist the readers to attain a clearer understanding of what sentiments ought to be entertained respecting the whole system of civil administration, if we enter on a discussion of each branch of it. These are three: The magistrate, who is the guardian and conservator of the laws: The laws, according to which he governs: The people, who are governed by the laws, and obey the magistrate. Let us, therefore, examine, first, the function of a magistrate, whether it be a legitimate calling and approved by God, the nature of the duty, and the extent of the power; secondly, by what laws Christian government ought to be regulated; and lastly, what advantage the people derive from the laws, and what obedience they owe to the magistrate.

(2) THE FUNCTION AND AUTHORITY
OF CIVIL RULERS

The Lord has not only testified that the function of magistrates has his approbation and acceptance, but has eminently commended it to us, by dignifying it with the most honourable titles. . . . No doubt ought . . . to be entertained by any person that civil magistracy is a calling not only holy and legitimate, but far the most sacred and honourable in human life. . . . This consideration ought continually to occupy the magistrates themselves, since it is calculated to furnish them with a powerful stimulus, by which they may be excited to their duty, and to afford them peculiar consolation, by which the difficulties of their office, which certainly are many and arduous, may be alleviated. For what an ardent pursuit of integrity, prudence, clemency, moderation, and innocence ought they to prescribe to themselves, who are conscious of having been constituted ministers of the Divine justice! With what confidence will they admit iniquity to their tribunal, which they understand to be the throne of the living God? With what audacity will they pronounce an unjust sentence with that mouth which they know to be the destined organ of Divine truth? With what conscience will they subscribe to impious decrees with that hand which they know to be appointed to register the edicts of God? In short, if they remember that they are the vicegerents of God, it behoves them to watch with all care, earnestness, and diligence, that in their administration they may exhibit to men an image, as it were, of the providence, care, goodness, benevolence, and justice of God. . . . If they fail in their duty, they not only injure men by criminally distressing them, but even offend God by polluting his sacred judgments. . . .

For private men, who have no authority to deliberate on the regulation of any public affairs, it would surely be a vain occupation to dispute which would be the best form of government in the

IV. xx. 4

IV. xx. 6

IV. xx. 8

place where they live. Besides, this could not be simply determined, as an abstract question, without great impropriety, since
the principle to guide the decision must depend on circumstances.
And even if we compare the different forms together, without
their circumstances, their advantages are so nearly equal, that it
will not be easy to discover óf which the utility preponderates. The
forms of civil government are considered to be of three kinds:
Monarchy, which is the dominion of one person, whether called a
king, or a duke, or any other title; Aristocracy, or the dominion
of the principal persons of a nation; and Democracy, or popular
government, in which the power resides in the people at large.
It is true that the transition is easy from monarchy to despotism;
it is not much more difficult from aristocracy to oligarchy, or the
faction of a few; but it is most easy of all from democracy to
sedition. Indeed, if these three forms of government, which are
stated by philosophers, be considered in themselves, I shall by no
means deny, that either aristocracy, or a mixture of aristocracy
and democracy, far excels all others; and that indeed not of itself,
but because it very rarely happens that kings regulate themselves
so that their will is never at variance with justice and rectitude;
or, in the next place, that they are endued with such penetration
and prudence, as in all cases to discover what is best. The vice or
imperfection of men therefore renders it safer and more tolerable
for the government to be in the hands of many, that they may
afford each other mutual assistance and admonition, and that if
any one arrogate to himself more than is right, the many may act
as censors and masters to restrain his ambition. . . .

I readily acknowledge that no kind of government is more
happy than this, where liberty is regulated with becoming moderation, and properly established on a durable basis, so also I consider those as the most happy people, who are permitted to enjoy
such a condition; and if they exert their strenuous and constant
efforts for its preservation and retention, I admit that they act in
perfect consistence with their duty. And to this object the magistrates likewise ought to apply their greatest diligence, that they
suffer not the liberty, of which they are constituted guardians, to
be in any respect diminished, much less to be violated: if they are
inactive and unconcerned about this, they are perfidious to their

office, and traitors to their country. But if those, to whom the will
of God has assigned another form of government, transfer this to
themselves so as to be tempted to desire a revolution, the very
thought will be not only foolish and useless, but altogether criminal. If we limit not our views to one city, but look round and take
a comprehensive survey of the whole world, or at least extend our
observations to distant lands, we shall certainly find it to be a
wise arrangement of Divine Providence that various countries are
governed by different forms of civil polity; for they are admirably
held together with a certain inequality, as the elements are com-
bined in very unequal proportions. . . .

Here it is necessary to state in a brief manner the nature of the   IV. xx. 9
office of magistracy, as described in the word of God, and wherein
it consists. If the Scripture did not teach that this office extends
to both tables of the law, we might learn it from heathen writers;
for not one of them has treated of the office of magistrates, of legislation, and civil government, without beginning with religion and
Divine worship. And thus they have all confessed that no government can be happily constituted, unless its first object be the promotion of piety and that all laws are preposterous which neglect
the claims of God, and merely provide for the interests of men.
. . . With respect to the second table, Jeremiah admonishes kings
in the following manner: "Execute ye judgment and righteousness, and deliver the spoiled out of the hand of the oppressor;
and do no wrong, do no violence to the stranger, the fatherless,
nor the widow, neither shed innocent blood." (y) . . . We see,
therefore, that they are constituted the protectors and vindicators
of the public innocence, modesty, probity, and tranquillity, whose
sole object it ought to be to promote the common peace and security of all. . . . *Righteousness* means the care, patronage, defence, vindication, and liberation of the innocent: *judgment* imports the repression of the audacity, the coercion of the violence,
and the punishment of the crimes, of the impious. . . .

Here . . . arises an important and difficult question. If by the   IV. xx. 10
law of God all Christians are forbidden to kill, (e) . . . how can
it be compatible with piety for magistrates to shed blood? But if

---

(y) Jer. xxii. 3.   (e) Exod. xx. 13.

we understand, that in the infliction of punishments, the magistrate does not act at all from himself, but merely executes the judgments of God, we shall not be embarrassed with this scruple. . . . Yet it behoves the magistrate to be on his guard against . . . these errors; that he do not, by excessive severity, wound rather than heal; or, through a superstitious affectation of clemency, fall into a mistaken humanity, which is the worst kind of cruelty, by indulging a weak and ill-judged lenity, to the detriment of multitudes. . . .

IV. xx. 11   Now, as it is sometimes necessary for kings and nations to take up arms for the infliction of such public vengeance, the same reason will lead us to infer the lawfulness of wars which are undertaken for this end. For if they have been intrusted with power to preserve the tranquillity of their own territories, to suppress the seditious tumults of disturbers, to succour the victims of oppression, and to punish crimes, — can they exert this power for a better purpose, than to repel the violence of him who disturbs both the private repose of individuals and the general tranquillity of the nation; who excites insurrections, and perpetrates acts of oppression, cruelty, and every species of crime? If they ought to be the guardians and defenders of the laws, it is incumbent upon them to defeat the efforts of all by whose injustice the discipline of the laws is corrupted. And if they justly punish those robbers, whose injuries have only extended to a few persons, shall they suffer a whole district to be plundered and devastated with impunity? For there is no difference, whether he, who in a hostile manner invades, disturbs, and plunders the territory of another to which he has no right, be a king, or one of the meanest of mankind: all persons of this description are equally to be considered as robbers, and ought to be punished as such. It is the dictate both of natural equity, and of the nature of the office, therefore, that princes are armed, not only to restrain the crimes of private individuals by judicial punishments, but also to defend the territories committed to their charge by going to war against any hostile aggression; and the Holy Spirit, in many passages of Scripture, declares such wars to be lawful.

IV. xx. 12   If it be objected that the New Testament contains no precept or example, which proves war to be lawful to Christians, I answer, first, that the reason for waging war which existed in ancient times, is equally valid in the present age; and that, on the contrary, there is no cause to prevent princes from defending their subjects. Secondly, that no express declaration on this subject is to be expected in the writings of the apostles, whose design was, not to organize civil governments, but to describe the spiritual kingdom of Christ. Lastly, that in those very writings it is implied by the way, that no change has been made in this respect by the coming of Christ. . . . But here all magistrates ought to be very cautious, . . . if arms are to be resorted to against an enemy, that is, an armed robber, they ought not to seize a trivial occasion, nor even to take it when presented, unless they are driven to it by extreme necessity. For . . . certainly we ought to make every other attempt before we have recourse to the decision of arms. . . . Moreover, on this right of war depends the lawfulness of garrisons, alliances, and other civil munitions. By *garrisons*, I mean soldiers who are stationed in towns to defend the boundaries of a country. By *alliances*, I mean confederations which are made between neighbouring princes, that, if any disturbance arise in their territories, they will render each other mutual assistance, and will unite their forces together for the common resistance of the common enemies of mankind. By *civil munitions*, I mean all the provisions which are employed in the art of war.

In the last place, I think it necessary to add, that tributes and taxes are the legitimate revenues of princes; which, indeed, they ought principally to employ in sustaining the public expenses of their office, but which they may likewise use for the support of their domestic splendour, which is closely connected with the dignity of the government that they hold. . . . On the other hand, princes themselves ought to remember, that their finances are not so much private incomes, as the revenues of the whole people, according to the testimony of Paul, (y) and therefore cannot be lavished or dilapidated without manifest injustice; or, rather, that they are to be considered as the blood of the people, not to spare which is the most inhuman cruelty; and their various imposts and tributes ought to be regarded merely as aids of the public neces-

IV. xx. 13

(y) Rom. xiii. 6.

sity, to burden the people with which, without cause, would be tyrannical rapacity. These things give no encouragement to princes to indulge profusion and luxury. . . .

(3) THE NATURE OF CIVIL LAWS

IV. xx. 14   From the magistracy, we next proceed to the laws, which are the strong nerves of civil polity, or, according to an appellation which Cicero has borrowed from Plato, the *souls of states*, without which magistracy cannot subsist, as, on the other hand, without magistrates laws are of no force. No observation, therefore, can be more correct than this, that the law is a silent magistrate, and a magistrate a speaking law. . . .

IV. xx. 15   All nations are left at liberty to enact such laws as they shall find to be respectively expedient for them; provided they be framed according to that perpetual rule of love, so that, though they vary in form, they may have the same end. . . .

IV. xx. 16   The objection made by some, that it is an insult to the law of God given by Moses, when it is abrogated, and other laws are preferred to it, is without any foundation; for neither are other laws preferred to it, when they are more approved, not on a simple comparison, but on account of the circumstances of time, place, and nation; nor do we abrogate that which was never given to us. For the Lord gave not that law by the hand of Moses to be promulgated among all nations, and to be universally binding; but after having taken the Jewish nation into his special charge, patronage, and protection, he was pleased to become, in a peculiar manner, their legislator, and, as became a wise legislator, in all the laws which he gave them, he had a special regard to their peculiar circumstances.

(4) THE CHRISTIAN ATTITUDE
TOWARD THE STATE

IV. xx. 17   It now remains for us . . . to examine what advantage the common society of Christians derives from laws, judgments, and magistrates; with which is connected another question — what honour private persons ought to render to magistrates, and how far their

IV. xx. 18   obedience ought to extend. . . . Judicial processes are lawful to those who use them rightly; and . . . the right use, both for the plaintiff and for the defendant, is this: First, if the plaintiff, being injured either in his person or in his property, has recourse to the protection of the magistrate, states his complaint, makes a just and equitable claim, but without any desire of injury or revenge, without any asperity or hatred, without any ardour for contention, but rather prepared to waive his right, and to sustain some disadvantage, than to cherish enmity against his adversary. Secondly, if the defendant, being summoned, appears on the day appointed, and defends his cause by the best arguments in his power, without any bitterness, but with the simple desire of maintaining his just right. On the contrary, when their minds are filled with malevolence, corrupted with envy, incensed with wrath, stimulated with revenge, or inflamed with the fervour of contention, so as to diminish their charity, all the proceedings of the justest cause are inevitably wicked. For it ought to be an established maxim with all Christians, that however just a cause may be, no lawsuit can ever be carried on in a proper manner by any man, who does not feel as much benevolence and affection towards his adversary, as if the business in dispute had already been settled and terminated by an amicable adjustment. Some, perhaps, will object, that such moderation in lawsuits is far from being ever practised, and that if one instance of it were to be found, it would be regarded as a prodigy. I confess, indeed, that, in the corruption of these times, the example of an upright litigator is very rare; but the thing itself ceases not to be good and pure, if it be not defiled by an adventitious evil. But when we hear that the assistance of the magistrate is a holy gift of God, it behoves us to use the more assiduous caution that it be not contaminated by our guilt. . . .

The first duty of subjects towards their magistrates is to enter- IV. xx. 22
tain the most honourable sentiments of their function, which they know to be a jurisdiction delegated to them from God, and on that account to esteem and reverence them as God's ministers and vicegerents. . . . I am not speaking of the persons, as if the mask of dignity ought to palliate or excuse folly, ignorance, or cruelty, and conduct the most nefarious and flagitious, and so to acquire for vices the praise due to virtues; but I affirm that the station itself is worthy of honour and reverence; so that, whoever our

governors are, they ought to possess our esteem and veneration on account of the office which they fill.

IV. xx. 23   Hence follows another duty, that, with minds disposed to honour and reverence magistrates, subjects approve their obedience to them, in submitting to their edicts, in paying taxes, in discharging public duties, and bearing burdens which relate to the common defence, and in fulfilling all their other commands. . . . Under this obedience I also include the moderation which private persons ought to prescribe to themselves in relation to public affairs, that they do not, without being called upon, intermeddle with affairs of state, or rashly intrude themselves into the office of magistrates, or undertake any thing of a public nature. If there be any thing in the public administration which requires to be corrected, let them not raise any tumults, or take the business into their own hands, which ought to be all bound in this respect, but let them refer it to the cognizance of the magistrate, who is alone authorized to regulate the concerns of the public. I mean, that they ought to attempt nothing without being commanded; for when they have the command of a governor, then they also are invested with public authority. . . .

IV. xx. 24   Now, as we have hitherto described a magistrate who truly answers to his title; who is the father of his country, and, as the poet calls him, the pastor of his people, the guardian of peace, the protector of justice, the avenger of innocence; he would justly be deemed insane who disapproved of such a government. But, as it has happened, in almost all ages, that some princes, regardless of every thing to which they ought to have directed their attention and provision, give themselves up to their pleasures in indolent exemption from every care; others, absorbed in their own interest, expose to sale all laws, privileges, rights, and judgments; others plunder the public of wealth, which they afterwards lavish in mad prodigality; others commit flagrant outrages, pillaging houses, violating virgins and matrons, and murdering infants; many persons cannot be persuaded that such ought to be acknowledged as princes, whom, as far as possible, they ought to obey. For in such enormities, and actions so completely incompatible, not only with the office of a magistrate, but with the duty of every man, they discover no appearance of the image of God, which ought to be conspicuous in a magistrate; while they perceive no vestige of that minister of God who is " not a terror to good works, but to the evil," who is sent "for the punishment of evil-doers, and for the praise of them that do well; " nor recognize that governor, whose dignity and authority the Scripture recommends to us. And certainly the minds of men have always been naturally disposed to hate and execrate tyrants as much as to love and reverence legitimate kings.

But, if we direct our attention to the word of God, it will carry us much further; even to submit to the government, not only of those princes who discharge their duty to us with becoming integrity and fidelity, but of all who possess the sovereignty, even though they perform none of the duties of their function. For, though the Lord testifies that the magistrate is an eminent gift of his liberality to preserve the safety of men, and prescribes to magistrates themselves the extent of their duty, yet he at the same time declares, that whatever be their characters, they have their government only from him; that those who govern for the public good are true specimens and mirrors of his beneficence; and that those who rule in an unjust and tyrannical manner are raised up by him to punish the iniquity of the people; that all equally possess that sacred majesty with which he has invested legitimate authority. . . . IV. xx. 25

We owe these sentiments of affection and reverence to all our rulers, whatever their characters may be; which I the more frequently repeat, that we may learn not to scrutinize the persons themselves, but may be satisfied with knowing that they are invested by the will of the Lord with that function, upon which he has impressed an inviolable majesty. But it will be said, that rulers owe mutual duties to their subjects. That I have already confessed. But he who infers from this that obedience ought to be rendered to none but just rulers, is a very bad reasoner. For husbands owe mutual duties to their wives, and parents to their children. Now, if husbands and parents violate their obligations; if parents conduct themselves with discouraging severity and fastidious moroseness towards their children, whom they are forbidden to provoke to wrath; (d) if husbands despise and vex their wives, whom they IV. xx. 29

(d) Ephes. vi. 1.   Col. iii. 21.

are commanded to love and to spare as the weaker vessels; (e) does it follow that children should be less obedient to their parents, or wives to their husbands? . . . If we are inhumanly harassed by a cruel prince; if we are rapaciously plundered by an avaricious or luxurious one; if we are neglected by an indolent one; or if we are persecuted, on account of piety, by an impious and sacrilegious one, — let us first call to mind our transgressions against God, which he undoubtedly chastises by these scourges. Thus our impatience will be restrained by humility. Let us, in the next place, consider that it is not our province to remedy these evils, and that nothing remains for us, but to implore the aid of the Lord, in whose hand are the hearts of kings and the revolutions of kingdoms. It is " God " who " standeth in the congregation of the mighty," and " judgeth among the gods." (f) . . .

IV. xx. 30   And here is displayed his wonderful goodness, and power, and providence; for sometimes he raises up some of his servants as public avengers, and arms them with his commission to punish unrighteous domination, and to deliver from their distressing calamities a people who have been unjustly oppressed: sometimes he accomplishes this end by the fury of men who meditate and attempt something altogether different. . . .

IV. xx. 32   But in the obedience which we have shown to be due to the authority of governors, it is always necessary to make one exception, and that is entitled to our first attention, — that it do not seduce us from obedience to him, to whose will the desires of all kings ought to be subject, to whose decrees all their commands ought to yield, to whose majesty all their sceptres ought to submit. And, indeed, how preposterous it would be for us, with a view to satisfy men, to incur the displeasure of him on whose account we yield obedience to men! The Lord, therefore, is the King of kings; who, when he has opened his sacred mouth, is to be heard alone, above all, for all, and before all; in the next place, we are subject to those men who preside over us; but no otherwise than in him. If they command any thing against him, it ought not to have the least attention; nor, in this case, ought we to pay any regard to all that dignity attached to magistrates; to which no injury is done when it is subjected to the unrivalled and supreme power of God.

(e) Ephes. v. 25.   1 Pet. iii. 7.   (f) Psalm lxxxii. 1.

INDEX

This index has been prepared in loyalty to Calvin's terminology and as a guide to the possible present-day application of his teaching. The first three references are to the book, chapter, and section of THE INSTITUTES. The page references are to this Compend.

SCRIPTURE REFERENCES

228   SCRIPTURE REFERENCES